Ashes
No
More

Ashes No More

by

ASHLEY BROOKE

A MEMOIR

BRENTWOOD

PO BOX #2583
Brentwood, TN 37024

This book is a memoir. It reflects the author's present recollections of experiences over time, medical records, and journal entries. It is written with self-reflection, humor, and slight embarrassment. Some names, conversations, and characteristics have been changed, and characters and events combined, compressed, and reordered.

Printed in the United States of America.

First edition: 2024
10 9 8 7 6 5 4 3 2 1

ISBN: 979-8-218-35781-8 (Paperback)
ISBN: 979-8-218-35782-5 (E-book)

Publisher's Cataloging-in-Publication Data

Names: Brooke, Ashley, author.
Title: Ashes no more / by Ashley Brooke.
Description: Includes bibliographical references. | Nashville, TN: Babysitting Money, 2024.
Identifiers: ISBN: 979-8-218-35781-8 (paperback) | 979-8-218-35782-5 (e-book)
Subjects: LCSH Brooke, Ashley. | Comedians--Biography. | Adult child sexual abuse victims--Biography. | Adult child abuse victims--Rehabilitation--Biography. | Recovered memory--Biography. | Christian biography. | BISAC BIOGRAPHY & AUTOBIOGRAPHY / Memoirs | BIOGRAPHY & AUTOBIOGRAPHY / Religious | BIOGRAPHY & AUTOBIOGRAPHY / Entertainment & Performing Arts
Classification: LCC RC569.5 .B76 2024| DDC 616.85/092--dc23

Cover design by Jared Collins at JaredGraphics
Back cover photo by Nora Canfield
About the Author photo by Nora Canfield

To all the little girls who are afraid of the dark.

CONTENTS

CONTENTS

FOREWORD

Trauma leaves its mark, even when it cannot be seen. Our ways of coping after experiencing trauma in key developmental years can become so habitual that we no longer notice them as coping, and they instead become our normal. Remaining activated and guarded in our bodies, or in chronic fight or flight, is an example of this process. We pay a tax for it over time. The constant activation of the sympathetic nervous system (SNS) affects how the body attempts to regulate itself. The SNS perceives danger and prepares the body to respond. It is designed as a temporary escalation of our nervous system to promote survival. When a threat never leaves, the body works to continue to protect us. Our bodies become fatigued and worn down and begin to show signs of wear and tear. Pains develop. Sleep suffers. And we still are not regulated. Emotionally and relationally, we pay a different price. Powerful and intense negative emotions arise, often without external support, such as trusting supportive relationships and internal resources, to help work through or control them. We can experience difficulties developing trust in relationships, unhealthy attachment patterns, or destructive behavior. As you read Ashley's story, you may begin to recognize the marks of trauma. Slowly, as more information comes to light, the story rewrites itself from a trauma-informed lens. What once was labeled as "dramatic behavior" takes on new meaning.

Ashley and I met in 2017, when I walked into a urology clinic room where she had routine outpatient care addressing chronic bladder and urinary symptoms. Ashley, having been treated for interstitial cystitis for nearly two decades, was surprised to see a psychologist. She joked with the nurse practitioner, whom she knew extremely well. She was a comedian with a dry, quick-witted, and sometimes dark sense of humor. Over the course of forty-five minutes, Ashley openly discussed her bladder condition and its varying levels of severity. During unpredictable symptom exacerbations, the pain had her bedridden or urinating every fifteen minutes. She was warm and engaging, and at the same time did not believe her pain could improve. Her resignation was understandable. At the time, she had a device surgically implanted to help with urinary symptoms, which in fact did not help. She was actively engaged in physical therapy and psychotherapy, made dietary changes, meditated daily, and took medicines as prescribed. Ashley had been through just about every available medicine or procedure at that point outside of having her bladder removed entirely. Through flashes of hopelessness, she expressed a commitment to try anything that might help her pain—even guided imagery and relaxation-based pain interventions.

To Ashley's complete shock, reducing physiological tension through these interventions helped. It helped so much that at times she had no pain. She was not cured per se, but better. This sparked a mix of curiosity and disbelief. Twenty years of pain. Did she really carry that much tension? What causes it? How does it go away? Is it reversible? Ashley spoke more openly about traumatic experiences she endured as a young adult. Ashley discerned that as her stress increased, her symptoms worsened. And sometimes, her symptoms would worsen completely out of the blue and become quickly debilitating. Her condition was difficult to manage and frustrating, particularly because when she experienced some relief, she wanted more. To understand. To help her body. She worked her way out of a difficult relationship and symptoms further improved. This led to a yearslong internal journey to better understand how traumatic life experiences and relational dynamics could affect her health and bladder, even decades later.

Recently, missing pieces of Ashley's story emerged. As you will learn when reading, finding missing pieces of our past rewrites our whole life narrative. We see ourselves in a new light and understand our behaviors differently. As the reader, you will reflect on earlier parts of Ashley's story and rewrite it together, developing both compassion and respect for how and what she survived. Ashley's journey took extreme courage and bravery to learn about what happened, face it, and now share it with the world.

Per Dr. Judith Lewis Herman, one of the most influential trauma psychologists of our time, trauma recovery generally follows three phases: The first involves creating a sense of safety in the body and stabilizing one's world. Second comes remembering what happened and processing traumatic memories. Doing so is often accompanied by overwhelming grief and sadness, both for what happened and for what was lost or missed out on in life. The third phase is reconnecting with people, meaningful experiences, and oneself. At this point, trauma becomes integrated as a *part* of us—not something we can forget, disavow, or run from (however hard we may have tried). One challenge that integration poses is deriving meaning from one's experiences. Meaning making can take shape through giving back or trauma advocacy. To transform her suffering and give back to others, Ashley chose to write.

There are some experiences in life filled with such horror and evil, there aren't words to describe them. We label them as "unspeakable." Ashley has found a way to walk you, the reader, through places where there are no words. Through humor, empathy, and relatability, she has given voice to the unspeakable. As the modern psychoanalyst Michael Eigen wrote, "Deep lines cut by trauma provide access to depths that are otherwise unreachable. In such instances, nourishment follows trauma to new places. We wish things could be otherwise . . . easier. But we have little choice when illumination shines through injury." In illuminating her story, Ashley continues to heal, brings connection to survivors, and may inspire others to find the courage to keep going and never stop searching.

Lindsey C. McKernan, PhD, MPH
Associate Professor of Psychiatry and Behavioral Sciences
Vanderbilt University Medical Center

"I have endured a lot of abuse in my life. It began in my childhood. I am beginning to believe that throughout my years of counseling, I have missed a memory somewhere or that the Lord hasn't revealed it to me yet. There still may be a rock left unturned. My previous relationships teach me that. If I were completely free from abuse, I don't believe abusers would find me so appealing."
Ashley Brooke, July 19, 2021[1]

PART 1

BEFORE I REMEMBER

CHAPTER 1

THE GREAT
ESCAPE ARTIST

"It's Alzheimer's," my mother abruptly announces to me over the phone.

I stare into my laptop; my mind goes blank . . . so much blankness. We found out in September that Dad had dementia. Today I find out it is Alzheimer's. I want to believe it is only dementia, just plain old dementia. Alzheimer's sounds like more of a death sentence. It's like the difference between varsity and junior varsity; one you take a little more seriously.

"Okay, Mom. We'll get through it," I reply.

"Alright, I'll talk to you later," she said, hanging up.

I feel a knot inside my stomach. It swells, reaching up to my throat. My nostrils flare, and the knot comes out of my eyes in the form of tears. I am hysterical and angry. I have been telling her for years he was showing the signs. She would call them "senior moments," but I knew these were more than moments.

My father's mother had Alzheimer's. I never knew her without it. She lived in a nursing home in Pennsylvania where we would visit when I was young, and she was a large woman confined to a wheelchair. She would swear her roommate, Dorothy, locked her into her closet at night. It was the first time I watched someone believe their own lie.

My father would say, "Mom, where's Dorothy now?"

To which she would laugh and respond, "Dorothy is in Oz!"

And then she would pet a stuffed cat on her lap and stare at my father as if she had no clue in the world who he was. From outside her room, I'd hear wailing and yelling from the other residents. I would pray, "God, please don't ever let this happen to me." And now it is happening to my father.

Within months of his diagnosis, we move my father into memory care. He settles in nicely at first, convinced this is his new place of employment. When I call, he rushes me off the phone like he did before he was sick. Some days when I visit him, he is exasperated and overwhelmed by his "meetings." He becomes an escape artist. He breaks out of his unit and one day makes his way to the other side of the parking lot. Another time, he makes it outside and sits on a bench. When he's found, he insists he is waiting for my mother and me to pick him up from work. Another time, he is caught coming off the elevator. Like a felon, he is given an ankle monitor. He's always been incredibly sneaky. The Alzheimer's doesn't change this. I, on the other hand, feel very, very sick.

Despite how I feel, I drag myself out of bed to take my father to chapel. I am running late and struggle my way off the elevator and down the hall to get my father. I open his door.

"Come on, Dad. Let's go. We are late," I say, gasping for air.

"Where are we going?" he asks.

"Chapel, Dad. I take you to the chapel here every Sunday."

"Okay, let me grab my hat."

"Does anyone have any prayer requests?" the preacher asks. Desperate, I raise my hand. "Please pray for me. I am having health problems." I open the Bible and follow along with the preacher's teaching.

My father stares vacantly at the church program in his hand. "I gotta go pee."

"Okay, Dad. Let's go pee." I take my father down the hall to use the bathroom and wait for him outside the door.

We return to the service, and he complains, "Let's get out of here."

"We'll leave when the preacher's done."

I feel like I'm raising a five-year-old. The service finishes, and I take my father back to his unit and into his dining hall. Like always, I go into his apartment to wait for him to finish his lunch. This time I take a nap in his bed. I am in a deep sleep when I hear the doorknob turn and my father's footsteps. I shoot straight out of the bed. It alarms me how quickly I jump awake. "Ashes, you can go back to sleep. It's okay."

"No, that's okay, Dad." Sleeping in his bedroom with him in the other room feels uncomfortable to me. I sit down on his couch and listen to him complain about my mother. Today, he is convinced she has a new boyfriend. Last week she was dead, and the week before that, she was a lesbian.

I cut the TV on, and *Golden Girls* is on. I listen as Rose tells Blanche to "never ever give up on your dreams, even when they're doused in sorrow, because even though they seem far away, they could come true tomorrow."[2] I understand Blanche's pain. I wish my dreams would come true too. I wish I was on that TV and not in this memory care. Then again, if my dreams did come true tomorrow, I would probably need a cortisone shot to get me out of bed. I have a choice. *I can let the pain in my heart break me, or I can break through.*

Later that week, I get a text message from my good friends, Dusty and Hannah, congratulating me. I have been voted one of the top three comedians in my city by a local magazine. This is unbelievable. I've been performing standup for twelve years, and I finally have my first credit. All those hours of performing in empty bars and responding to strange men in DMs (direct messages) on social media are paying off. I can't wait to celebrate and buy myself some new shoes.

As with every high of my life, there is a low. I've received recognition, but I also feel so sick I can hardly move. *Not again.* I've spent my entire life sick and heartbroken. The doctors prescribe their medications, they run their tests, they do their surgeries, and everything always comes back normal. There's never an answer as to why I become so ill. My immune tests always come back intact. There's something very wrong with me. I know it. I pray to the Lord to reveal what it is. I feel deep in my spirit that it's not something the doctors are going to find. It is something I will find, and once I find it, *I can break through.*

PART 2

AS IT WAS HAPPENING

CHAPTER 2

THE QUEEN OF SHEBA

Little girls should be playing hopscotch and jumping rope, having fun without a care in the world other than picking their favorite ice cream off a truck. Little girls should be on playgrounds, not in hospitals and clinics, like me.

The first time I have surgery, I am five years old. Plagued with bladder infections, I've been wetting my pants and my bed consistently for two years, despite being fully potty-trained. My mother takes me to a urologist, who wants to perform a surgery and look inside my bladder. The nurses are so nice. Everything is hectic, and everyone moves around very quickly, but I feel safe and special. I feel seen. "You are going to go to sleep for a little while, and when you wake up, we will be here waiting for you," they tell me. I feel something cold press against my body. I feel a mask come toward my face, and I can smell its plastic.

When I wake up, I am told I must pee before I can leave the hospital. It burns. I do not like this at all and want to go home. My mother begins giving me medicine every morning. I hate it.

THE QUEEN OF SHEBA

I figure every child must take medicine, and one day, we don't need to take it anymore. I don't see myself as any different from my friends.

School is an exciting concept for a little girl. Little girls dream of becoming big girls, and big girls go to school. School is a rite of passage for a five-year-old girl. *First, it's school, then it's marriage. Easy peasy.* I start kindergarten in Catholic school. My mom packs me an extra pair of panties, some tights, and a jumper every day in case I have an accident. She always calls it an "accident" when I wet myself. I can never control it. It just happens.

My kindergarten classroom has a big bathroom in it. There is plenty of room for me to change comfortably on the accident days. There are two doors to the bathroom. One leads to my classroom, and one leads to another classroom. Sometimes I get nervous someone from the other door is going to open it and see me naked. Other than this, I love kindergarten. I love my cubby, and I love my backpack. I have a desk that looks like a table. My name is printed out on a card and sits in front of me, so everyone knows who I am. I get to sit by the teacher's desk. I feel safe close to her. Sometimes she turns toward me and gets a sad look on her face.

At night, my dad teaches me my letters. He lifts my shirt and draws letters on my back. I guess the letters, and we both get happy when I get the right letter. I never want him to stop.

My mother sits downstairs in our den watching TV. She loves the TV. My dad loves his computer. My sister, Laura, who is sixteen years older than me, loves to sit in her room and play her guitar. I love to sit in my room and play school with my dollies.

Before I go to bed, my father comes into my room to check on me, and as he leaves, he looks at the doorknob, then back at me. "Keep this door unlocked," he says to me. Confused, I nod my head.

Every family has secrets, and mine is no different. Our secret is that I am a very sick little girl, and no one seems to know why. I still get a lot of bladder infections, and I go to the doctor a lot. I call him "the pee-pee doctor." He pulls my shirt up and presses on my belly. I get nervous. He asks me if it hurts when he presses on my belly. Sometimes he will ask my mother and me a question: "How is everything at home?"

"Oh, it's good. Very good," my mother will tell him with a smile.

I miss a lot of school because of my infections. Nurses start coming into my house. I sit in my mom's big chair in our den. The nurses put a needle in the back of my hand, and a long tube comes out of it, connecting to a bag above me. They come to our house several times a week for a while.

Because my mother is a nurse, she gives me the IV medications herself when she is home. The nurses tell me I am strong even though I don't feel like it. I don't feel any different from other little girls. I only get a lot of bladder infections and I hurt sometimes, but it will go away when I grow up.

One of the boy nurses says to me, "You look like the Queen of Sheba in that big chair." I like him. I feel special—seen.

My mother wants a bigger closet, so my parents move their bedroom downstairs and turn part of their garage into a closet for her. My mother gets everything she wants. I want to grow up and have big closets too.

My parents move me and my sister into different rooms upstairs, and my old bedroom becomes my dad's computer room. I don't like being upstairs at night without my parents. I am afraid of the upstairs, and I am afraid of the dark. The house makes loud noises. "It's settling, Ashley," my mother reassures me.

I am afraid to sleep in my room at night. I stare up into the hallway from the bottom of the stairs, and my heart races. The stairs creak as my feet step on each one. I feel a heaviness exuding from behind each door of the bedrooms in the hallway, including my bedroom.

I can't sleep in my room; it scares me. There is something in my room, and it wants to hurt me. It comes into my room at night when I am asleep, and it wakes me up and scares me. Even with my nightlight, I am still afraid and cannot sleep.

I start sleeping on the couch in our den. I think this "thing" can still get me, so I sleep in a sleeping bag on the floor of my parents' bedroom. Eventually, my parents get an extra bed and move it into their walk-in closet for me to sleep in. There is something terrible happening up those stairs.

CHAPTER 3

THESE ARE THE DAYS OF MY LIFE

The day is easier than the night, but I don't like the days much either. The days remind me I am alone. I often feel trapped like an animal in a menagerie. I know there is a big world outside of my parents' house, but I don't know how to access it. They don't leave the house much, and my mother regularly tells me no when I ask to go to a friend's house. I sit in the bay window of our living room and watch cars drive up and down the hill that faces our house. I don't know where the cars are heading, but I wish they would take me with them.

Catholic parents get very excited when their children reach second grade. Second grade is when Catholic children receive their First Communion. All us kids fill up the church and stand in line to have a priest hand us bread and wine. It sounds illegal, but it's not. It's like a giant party for kids, but the kids don't really want to be there. We would rather be watching cartoons or playing Nintendo. I have a *The Little Mermaid* Nintendo game waiting for me after this.

My mother dresses me up in a white dress and a large crown. I look like a princess—a sleep-deprived princess like in the *Princess and the Pea*. My parents take me to get my picture taken. I ride in the back seat of my mother's gray Buick Skyhawk as we pull up to Sears. She parks the car, and I feel a wave of emotion hit me. I don't know what it is, but sadness consumes me. I feel something has changed in me; I am no longer a little girl. Something happened, and life will never be like it was before this day.

I am getting sicker. Sometimes it's a bladder infection, sometimes it's a sore throat, sometimes it's a belly ache, and sometimes it's a headache. "How's everything at home?" the doctor will ask my mother and me. "Everything is good. Real good," she will reply with that same smile.

My mother is a great pretender. She has two faces—either smiling or scary. She's always nice when she wears her makeup; then she's a good mommy. When I am sad and I cry, she holds me and pats my back. "Let it all out," she will say to me as I sob uncontrollably. Little girls cry. It's what we do.

Sometimes, she will let me sit in her chair with her, and she'll say, "The day will come when the two of us can't fit in this chair anymore!"

"No, Mommy! Never. I can't imagine a life where we aren't side by side."

But, when her makeup is off, she screams. She yells at me and calls me a "wild woman."

"ASHLEEEEEEYYYYY!" I can hear her yelling for me from the bottom of the stairs. I hold my breath in fear. "I'M COMING UP THERE," she threatens. I hear her feet stomp on the stairs. I start to hide. The door flings open. "WHERE ARE YOU?!"

"Mommy! No," I plead. There is no stopping her when she is this mad.

She grabs me, throws me on the floor, and sits on my back. "TELL ME YOU ARE SORRY," she demands.

"I'm sorry, Mommy. I'm sorry. I can't breathe," I cry, in between gasping for air. I don't always know what I have done, but I'll tell her anything she wants to hear so I can breathe again. She finally gets off me, and I struggle to catch my breath, sobbing uncontrollably as she leaves the room.

I don't understand why she gets so angry with me, and I don't understand why my father will not help me. He ignores the screaming and crying, burying his mind into his books.

I cling to her at times, desperate for her love. "Ashley, come on. Let me breathe a little. My God." She says she can't breathe, but I feel the only one dying is a part of me, who believes one day I will be good enough for my mother.

I think my mother hates me. I don't know why she hates me, but I know this isn't normal. As I get older, I fight her back. I "get fresh" with her, as she calls it.

Sometimes she locks me in my room. Other times she shuts down and ignores me. I sit on the floor next to her chair crying for her, begging for her to listen to me. She turns her head away from me. Her silence hurts.

Once she starts ignoring me, there is nothing I can do. I can't win her over. She leaves her chair, goes into her bedroom, slams her door, and locks herself in her room. I stand outside of it and beg her to open it and forgive me.

One day, I get a bright idea. I write her a note telling her how sorry I am and slide it under her door. She likes that. I am thrilled when I hear the door crack open. Now she is a good mommy.

Some mothers have other mothers watch their children after school. My mother shuffles me around from one classmate's house to another. I never like it. I feel like I'm outside looking into someone else's happy family. Some of the mothers watch *Days of Our Lives* and *The Young and the Restless*. I love to watch the drama. I want to grow up and be on that TV.

One of my babysitters has a daughter and a son, and I befriend her daughter. We play school and dress-up in her room. One day, she leaves me in her room as she runs to the kitchen to grab some snacks. While she is gone, her older brother comes into the room and corners me onto her bed. I try to get away from him and head toward the door, but his friend stands in front of it, blocking me. They laugh at me as I try to break away. I know he wants something bad from me, and I feel very afraid. His sister comes back into the room, and the two boys leave.

When I get home, I cry and cry. I tell my mother what happened, and she accuses me of lying. I stay up all night, distressed. As I make my way into the bathroom, sobbing uncontrollably, my sister wakes up and holds me, telling me I am safe.

My mother storms into the bathroom, and she's definitely not wearing makeup. "Mom, she's not making it up. Something happened. She's scared," my sister says.

"Fine. I will call the babysitter tomorrow," she says, with steam coming out of her ears. The next day before school, I expect her to tell me I don't ever have to go back to that horrible babysitter's house, and I can watch soap operas by myself. Instead, she informs me she talked to the babysitter, who assured my mother she would talk to the boys, and it would never happen again. I promise her I will be a good girl if she lets me come home from school, and instead, she makes me go back.

There is some fun in my life—it's not all bad. I am enrolled in dance, where I get to be a ballerina, a tap dancer, a jazz dancer, and an acrobat. In my dance class, I am mostly trained to dance to Phil Collins's songs and Michael Jackson's "Rock with You." I first perform onstage at dance recitals, and I feel like a star.

In our town, we have a theme park where I go during the summers with my friends. It has everything a young girl could want—roller coasters, swings, musical acts, gift shops, and funnel cake. I love the swings. There's about a hundred of them, and they're all connected to a carousel. It takes me high up in the air, around and around. I love to look down at the park beneath my tiny feet. It reminds me of the opening scene of a movie, except in this movie, I am the star.

I daydream a lot that I am in the movies. I want to be an actress when I grow up. I like to pretend I am in a film adaptation of *Rapunzel* in which I am a beautiful princess locked away in her mother's castle. One day, I will let my hair down, and a handsome prince will save me from her, and all my dreams will come true. I record every episode of *The Mickey Mouse Club* and *Kids Incorporated*. I laugh at all their jokes. I memorize all their songs and dances for my concerts, performed in my parents' den for our couch.

My sister gets married and moves out of our mother's castle. She is finally free, but I am not. I distract myself with the TV and my Nintendo games. My mother wants me to be into sports, so I join a softball team. Some afternoons my father and I play catch in the backyard, but neither of my parents come to my games.

My father loves to play computer games. He will go into his computer room for hours playing his games. "Hey, Ashes. Come here. You gotta see this," my father calls for me. I walk into his computer room and see him smiling at the screen, laughing. "Here, look at this. It's so cool. Now, don't tell your mother I'm showing you this." I walk further into the room and see a tiny man on the screen walking onto a beach with two naked people. I feel uncomfortable, but my dad is laughing so it must be funny. "Here, pull up a chair."

I grab an extra chair and sit next to him and watch him play his game. It's called *Leisure Suit Larry*. I like watching the little man walk around, and I like watching my father laugh. My father tells me I can play the game too, and we play the game together. There are a lot of naked people in the game; sometimes they kiss, and sometimes they get on top of each other. My dad laughs, and so do I. I love spending time with my dad. He's not just my dad, he is my friend.

We play games, and we share secrets. When my mother's back is turned, he shares his Budweiser with me. "Wanna little sip to wet your whistle?" he'll ask. Of course, I do! I want anything my mother doesn't want me to have! My dad slips me twenty dollars sometimes and tells me, "Don't tell your mother." He gives me money, and then I get to go to the mall with my friends and buy pencil boxes. I love pencil boxes! What did children do before God made Hello Kitty?

CHAPTER 4

YOU BE A GOOD GIRL

Puberty comes into my life like a tidal wave. At first, it starts like a ripple in the ocean, and then it becomes so massively obvious that everyone in its midst runs away from me. I develop quickly.

The other kids notice what I've been trying so desperately to hide the past few years. My mother refuses to buy me bras. She insists an undershirt will suffice. It does not.

The girls in my class whisper about me behind my back and stop inviting me to their parties. The boys make fun of me and take turns throwing water balloons at my chest on the playground. My father makes comments I don't like. He calls me "pure sex," and when he sees me in a skirt, his eyes bug out of his head and he says, "Ow-chee-waa-waa!" I don't know what any of it means, but I know I don't like it. I look at my mother for help, and she turns her head away.

My father comes into my room at night and does awful things to me. I push him off me. He tells me, "Be quiet; you'll wake your mother up." Other times he tells me, "We *have* to do it." *I don't understand. Who is he answering to? Did she put him up to this? Who is behind this?* I lie on my bed, paralyzed from the horror and betrayal.

"Stop! They're wrong! Let me talk to them," I yell, but nothing comes out of my mouth. I can't move. I lie lifelessly on my checkered sheets. My arm drapes over the side of my bed as I stare into darkness. My mind goes blank until he gets up to leave. *Wait, come back. Tell me this didn't happen. Tell me I'm wrong.* Instead, he continues toward the door, looks back at me, and says, "Now, you be a good girl." The stairs creak underneath his feet as he makes his way back down the stairs. My room is a very scary place.

I don't understand my father. He confuses me like my mother does. Sometimes he's fun, sometimes he hurts me, and other times he's religious.

He drives my neighbor and me to school every morning. We started out listening to a popular local radio station. I sang along with Ace of Base, and the DJ would make inappropriate jokes. My dad would laugh, and I would cringe.

Now our rides to school change. He listens to a Christian radio show called *Turning Point*, hosted by Dr. David Jeremiah.[3] My father embarrasses me as he sings along with the jingle, "This could be your turning point . . . *turning point*," and then he makes a trumpet sound. I don't understand my father. He's becoming active in our church and reading books about God all the time now. He wants me to read his religious books too. I don't want anything to do with him or his religious books. I can't stand him.

I blame myself for what he does to me. I should have known better. Every father is capable of something like this. It's the daughter's job to not give him the wrong idea. I have led him on. I should have been more careful. I can't tell anyone. No one will believe me. No one will believe he does this to me, and no one will believe I don't want it.

I am already having problems at school. The girls don't want to be my friend anymore, and the boys humiliate me. If anyone ever finds out what my father does, I will have no one.

Somewhere in between the self-loathing and shame, I bury our biggest secret into the deep recesses of my mind, and I forget it ever happened. The memory is gone, but its torment lives on and grows inside me. And the house continues to make its loud noises as if summoning evil to live inside its walls.

PART 3

FORGETTING

CHAPTER 5

THE CHEERLEADING, ROLLER-SKATING, COUNTRY LINE DANCER

I don't choose to forget what my father does to me. My brain chooses for me. As a child, I can't handle the emotions of remembering his crimes from the night before. Disgusted, I cringe. I hate him for what he does to me, and I hate myself. People say they would never forget if something bad happened to them. I disagree. We all want to forget the things that bring us shame. Some of us are better at it because we had to train ourselves at a very young age to forget the terrible things happening to us. Our brains focus on one thing: *staying alive.*

After school, I spend endless hours on the phone with my friend, Kitty. We make lots of jokes. We put our TVs on the same channel, hit the mute button, and do voiceovers. This is especially fun whenever a Michael Jackson music video comes on VH1—comic genius.

On Fridays after school, my classmates and I go across the street to the skating rink and roller-skate until our parents pick us up. On Saturday nights, another skating rink becomes a dance floor and hosts country line dancing. Anyone who is anyone goes country line dancing on Saturday nights. I love it. I meet a boy at the skating rink, and he becomes my boyfriend. We spend hours talking on the phone after school. I want to marry him one day, and I tell him that. I may tell him that too much.

I become a cheerleader at school. I don't know anything about football or cheerleading, but I love *being* a cheerleader. I am a cheerleading and roller-skating country line dancer. One day, I will put it on my résumé. I love to practice my cheers, and I love comedy. I want to grow up and be on *Saturday Night Live (SNL)* and marry my roller-skating boyfriend, of course.

We have pep rallies at school, and I imitate Craig and Ariana from my favorite *SNL* sketch, and everyone laughs. "Who's that Spartan in my teepee?"[4]

"It's Ashley! It's Ashley!"

The coaches are mad I don't take cheerleading seriously and threaten to kick me off the squad. That's when I know it's funny. Funny is when the boys laugh and the women get mad. I love making people laugh. It makes me feel good about myself, and I feel seen.

When I am not home, I smile and make everyone laugh, but when I am home, I feel intense pain. It's a type of pain I can't explain to my friends. I don't know where it comes from, but I hate myself, and I want to die. I want the pain inside me to end. I cut myself to purge the pain. I want someone to help me make it stop. I want to go to heaven.

I grab a bottle of my mother's ibuprofen and swallow a handful of pills. I write a letter telling my parents I can't go on anymore, and I pray God takes me away in the night. I wake up to my mother sitting at the bottom of the stairs, talking on the phone. "Yes, my daughter's name is Ashley, and she tried to kill herself. She needs to be admitted."

What is happening? Why I am still here? I don't understand. Who is she talking to?

"Ashley, get ready. You are going to the hospital," she informs me.

"But Mom. I'm not sick."

CHAPTER 6

BAD MEDICINE

My mother admits me into a psychiatric ward for juveniles. It is a dark and empty place. Although there are several patients in the ward, it feels so vast and empty to me. It is very quiet. I am escorted into my windowless room and shown my new bathroom. The bathroom has two doors, each leading to another bedroom. There is no curtain or mirror. I am not allowed to shave my legs. Oddly, there is a chair for a nurse to sit in while she watches me shower. I am afraid of anyone seeing me naked. I don't want to be here. I want to go home, but not to my parents' house. I want to go to another home that doesn't exist.

There are two beds in my room—one for me and one for another girl. The nurses tell me she is my roommate. She's adopted, and she won't stop running away from home. "After this, it's juvie for me. It sucks here, but you get used to it," she tells me.

Another girl from the other side of the bathroom is my age, and she's pregnant. We aren't in high school yet. "Kill yourself? Why would you wanna do that? You're a cheerleader and you're blonde. If I looked like you, I'd have everything I wanted," she tells me.

I don't know how to explain to her why I feel the way I do because I don't understand it either. She tells me about her boyfriend and how much she misses him, and I relate. My boyfriend and I didn't work out. I'm going to fire the wedding planner as soon as I get out of here.

The other girls seem to have it worse than me. I feel guilty being in the hospital. I'm the only kid here who hasn't had any trouble with the law or isn't pregnant. We meet every day for group in a big room with windows at the top of the walls. They do that on purpose so no one can reach them. One day, a tall boy gets upset and jumps, trying to break a window and escape. They take him to see the doctor. There's another boy in our group who is in a gang. I've never been around a gang member before this. I feel like I am on the set of *Oprah* every day listening to these kids tell their stories.

"You get a Prozac! You get a Prozac! Every kid gets a Prozac!" *I don't belong here.* "When can I leave?" I ask my doctor.

"When you're better," he tells me.

I am having horrible headaches. The doctor runs an MRI and diagnoses me with a chemical imbalance. Now I need to take Prozac every day. *Great. More medicine for breakfast.*

My family comes to visit me, but first they talk to the doctor for what feels like an eternity in a big room outside the ward. My sister cries when she sees me. After several weeks of telling me I am not better yet, the doctor finally releases me and diagnoses me with major depression. I am now his patient and will visit him once a month for my medicine.

I feel free leaving the hospital, but I don't feel any better. I go back to school, and the kids tease me after they find out where I spent my summer. I beg my parents to let me switch schools. I want to go somewhere no one knows me. I also want to go to a school where I don't have to wear a uniform, making that my selling point.

"The uniform doesn't allow me to fully express myself. I want to wear whatever I want so I can feel like myself. The doctor says I need to feel like I can be myself," I say as I present my case. I could be a lawyer. Naturally, my mother opposes me, but my father convinces her. He seems to feel sorry for me. My parents enroll me in the middle of my eighth-grade year into a new school, and something incredible happens. I am *the new girl*.

CHAPTER 7

THE NEW GIRL

The new girl—every little girl wants to be her. She's mysterious. She's typically not any prettier than the old girls, but the novelty of her intrigues the boys. The other girls feel threatened by her. Some befriend her, and others ignore her. Being the new girl is like being granted immunity. She is untouchable, and for once, *she is me.*

I love my new school. It's a Christian school. I am shocked to find out not everyone in the world is Catholic. My new classmates ask me if I worship Mary. I have no idea what they are talking about. I've never paid attention to a single Mass a day of my life. I don't know what we believe. I do know I don't believe in uniforms and neither does this school. It seems to me we have a lot in common already.

There is something about my new school that seems happier—maybe it's the lighting. We have lockers, which makes me nervous because I've never used a locker. And we change our clothes for physical education, which makes me nervous too. I am afraid of anyone seeing me naked. I do my best to hide in a corner as I struggle to change without showing anything.

Some of the girls start a rumor I stuff my bra, but luckily, I make some friends who help me squash that rumor. I make lots of friends. The kids here love my jokes and my *SNL* impressions. I can't join the cheerleading squad here because I don't know how to do a back handspring, but that is okay. I am the funny girl, and it wins me a lot of friends.

On Wednesdays, we have Chapel in the gym. We all sing, and sometimes there's a speaker. One Wednesday, we have a magician come to Chapel. He does magic tricks and tells us jokes. He also tells us he wanted to kill himself when he was a kid, but then he met Jesus, and now he doesn't want to die anymore. Hearing his story makes me feel less alone. His name is Stephen, and I hope I can be like him one day.

I snag a new boyfriend, the quarterback of the varsity football team. Dreams are coming true for this eighth grader. I am going to marry him one day. We go on dates, he buys me gifts for Valentine's Day and Christmas, I meet his parents, and he meets mine. I am sure he is going to propose to me soon. He asks me to do *everything* with him but sex. I don't like it, but I am afraid to tell him no. I don't want him to break up with me. I am too young to lose two potential marriages.

It's the summer before ninth grade, and I sadly enter high school single. "*It's not working out,*" he tells me. He wants to keep his options open for high school. I am devastated. After *everything* I had done for him and with him.

My popularity takes a hit. I beg him to take me back, and he looks at me like he hates me. He tells his friends what I let him do to me, and I am humiliated. They tease me endlessly and call me names. I struggle to move on from the relationship and create a new identity for myself. The first year at my new school, I am the new girl and the quarterback's girlfriend. Now, I am the girl wearing the scarlet letter. I turn to alcohol.

CHAPTER 8

LIKE FATHER, LIKE BOYFRIEND

I love drinking, and I love drugs. My bladder does not love my new ways, and I do not care. I love getting high. Being high feels like a giant sigh. There's pain, and then there's the beautiful relief that only blacking out can give.

Luckily, God blesses my household with the internet, and I am back on the prowl. I sit behind my father's computer and message with the older boys in my school. I like the older boys. The boys in my class are too immature for me. I need a man—a tenth-grade man.

I first meet Alex at a party. He gives me a cigarette, and a couple months later, I give him my virginity. "There is no way you are a virgin," he says in an accusing tone. I promise him I am a virgin. I don't know why he would think I would lie about such a thing. He's always so paranoid.

Alex was in rehab at fourteen, and now at sixteen, he is rehabilitated from cocaine addiction; however, his recovery conveniently allows cheap alcohol. He chooses my friends and my vices for me. I am not allowed to use drugs, but I am allowed to drink. My drink of choice is Zima. If I drop a Jolly Rancher in it, it tastes like flavored Alka-Seltzer, and I love it. I have a very sophisticated palate. We spend most nights at his mother's house, and she lets us drink and smoke. With every breath I take and every move I make, Alex watches me. He's not just my boyfriend, he's the thought police, always ready to charge me with the crime of thinking for myself. He's Alex the Terrible.

My father and Alex get along. After his shifts at Best Buy, Alex comes to our house and plays chess with my father. He always shakes my father's hand, and they laugh together. When Alex is not with me, my father asks about him. They have a lot in common. They're two salesmen with a grin, a firm handshake, and a dirty joke on their lips.

I figure because I have given Alex my virginity, we will one day marry. We don't always get along. We have big fights. Sometimes I start them because I want attention, and sometimes he starts them. He gets mad when I tell him I smoke weed behind his back with my girlfriends. He calls me a junkie and tells me I can't hang out with my friends anymore. Sometimes I hit him. Sometimes he pins me to the ground, tells me I'm fat, and spits on me. I cry and beg him to forgive me. I am so afraid he will leave me.

Alex tells me he is cheating on me with a girl from his alternative school. "What? I don't understand," I sob, choking on my tears.

"Yeah, I don't want to be with you anymore. *It's not working out.* You should go home." Standing in his driveway, I scream and beg him to stay with me. My world feels like it is falling apart. He tells me to stop embarrassing myself. I drive by his house after school looking for her car every day like the stable sixteen-year-old girl I am. Her car is always in his driveway. She leaves me no choice. I egg her car, and I receive my closure.

I spend my sophomore and junior years of high school falling in and out of love. I break my own heart, and some boys break it too. It appears no one is coming to rescue me from my mother's castle after all. The other girls in my class don't have the same problems I do. They have stable juvenile relationships and coping skills.

CHAPTER 9

WHO'S THAT SPARTAN IN MY REHAB?

I don't like the person I am. I do my best to change. My mother introduces me to hair highlights. When I was twelve, I bleached my hair, and she called me a whore, but in high school, blonde is acceptable in my mother's eyes. She's not always a bad mom; sometimes she takes me shopping to Victoria's Secret and buys me matching bras and panties. My mother also introduces me to the tanning bed, and I form a new addiction: *perfection*. I get my nails done every two weeks, my hair highlighted every six weeks, and tan almost daily. A girl must always be ready to meet her future husband.

I have pushed away most of my female friendships. I prefer to be alone with my drugs. I take ecstasy every weekend, yet somehow, I hold down a job scooping ice cream. During the weekdays, I wake up in the morning, I take my bladder medication and then some medication not prescribed to me. I smoke weed on the drive to school. I make a stop at

Mrs. Winner's and grab a sweet tea and a chicken biscuit. I arrive to my first period Spanish class and nod off. *What are they putting in that sweet tea?*

I am called to the principal's office often. Sometimes it's because I am late, and other times it's because I "get fresh" with the teachers. One time, I get suspended from school because I throw a full Mountain Dew can at a boy's head after he calls me a whore and tells me, "No one would touch you with a ten-foot pole." I regularly sit in detention hall and clean the bleachers as penance.

"Ashley, you're causing problems in school. We believe you're on drugs. We've searched your locker," my principal tells me.

"Well, that was dumb. I don't keep anything in my locker. It's in my car," I stupidly admit. In my car, I have a cute tin box from Hello Kitty. Inside it is a quarter ounce of weed, my pipe, some rolling papers, a few hits of acid, and some methadone.

"We're going to need you to pass a drug test," he informs me. I'm hit with panic. I've always been a terrible test taker. Today is no different. I am in big trouble, and I know it. I might not be able to graduate. I need to get it together. Our school counselor reaches out to me. She cares about me, and I can tell. She believes my addiction is not my fault. I don't understand. *Whose fault could it be?* She must be mistaken. I am admitted to an intensive outpatient program.

I go to school every morning, and then after school I go to rehab. I meet some new friends. Everyone here likes me. The counselors tell me I hide my pain behind my humor. They teach us about codependency and enablement. My mother checks all these boxes. *Why isn't she here?*

They drug test us each week. I can't fail any more drug tests. I quit using drugs and turn to chocolates. It's a twenty-eight-day program, and I eat my way through it. I am told I need to start going to Alcoholics Anonymous (AA) meetings and am handed a sheet of paper to get signed at the meetings.

One night an older man about three seats away from me has a seizure during a meeting. I decide this isn't for me. Sobriety is a health risk. I only need a few weeks to get off drugs; I'll be fine. I am assigned a therapist to help me as I continue my "road to recovery." Of course, it is a dead-end road. After thirty days, I start smoking weed again.

My parents blame my latest boyfriend for my smoking. They don't want me to see him anymore because he's a runaway. My mother can't see his potential like I can. "Ashley, he is a fugitive! You are harboring a fugitive. You are not allowed to see him!"

"You can't stop me," I challenge her, and I am right. She can't stop me from seeing him. That is the state's job. Eventually, my beloved is taken into state custody. Our relationship has evolved from hiding in our friends' basements and smoking weed to becoming pen pals. We write each other regularly. I write about my failing grades, and he writes about how we are going to marry when we turn eighteen. It's very Shakespearean.

While he is away, I spiral back into drug addiction. Weed isn't enough for me. I turn back to harder drugs. I also turn back to cutting myself, which is a compulsion for me. I don't know where it comes from, but I want it to stop. I am filled with dread and fear I am going to really hurt myself. I reach out to my road-to-recovery therapist informing her of the U-turn I have made during our journey.

"I have been using, and I want to die. Something is wrong with me."

"Do you need help? Do you think you could hurt yourself?" she asks.

"I do. I really do. I need help," I cry.

I am admitted into the emergency room for suicidal ideation. I come clean and tell the doctors about the pills, the ecstasy, the weed, and the methadone. I'm back to my old ways. I admit I was only able to stay off drugs for thirty days, and my grades are dropping. I hate my life, and I don't know what is wrong with me. I want to cut myself all the time. I am admitted into the psychiatric ward, once again. This time, it's different—I am admitted with the adults. Some of the other patients stare off in a catatonic state and mumble to themselves as they sit in front of a TV watching the news. *I do not belong here. I hate the news.*

The doctors ask me what kind of stressors I have in my life. I explain my boyfriend is in state custody and I've got a wedding to plan. Of course, I am in distress. My life is worse than an after-school special. After three days, I am discharged. "Your daughter is not mentally ill. Your daughter is an addict. She needs an inpatient drug rehabilitation program," my doctor informs my parents.

I leave the psychiatric hospital, and my Romeo leaves state custody. He also leaves me for another girl. *How could he do this? I've already picked out our wedding party.* I am once again a woman scorned. I struggle to get closure, but nothing helps a woman move on from one bad romance like another bad romance.

37

The high school boys are not enough for me. Now I have graduated to dating men in their twenties. Men in their twenties have access to more drugs than high school boys. I get a new boyfriend. He's twenty-two, and he's a Christian. He tells me all the churches are teaching the Bible wrong. That's why he had to burn three of them down. Understandable.

He talks a lot about God and the Bible, but he also does a lot of drugs with me and my new friend, Neely. Neely is also in her early twenties. She laughs at all my jokes, and she covers her mouth each time she laughs. I find out it's because Neely is missing a lot of teeth.

There is a rumor she gets them pulled so she can get pain medication. She takes more medication than I do. I tell her I have a headache; she looks over at her multitude of pills, opens a bottle, and hands me one. "Here, take this. It'll knock that right out."

I don't know where she got her medical training, but I trust her. She lives in a trailer with her boyfriend in his parents' backyard with her three kids. She calls me family, and I feel like I have a home. I feel seen.

I'm months away from graduating, and I am strung out. The drugs are emotionally breaking me down. I've spent the weekend with my church-burning, Christian boyfriend and my new family, taking lots of ecstasy and Neely's prescription medication. I do not like the way I feel. I feel that familiar dread coming upon me like I want to die again. It's consuming me just like it did when I was young. I need help and I know it. It's time I follow the doctor's orders and go to an inpatient rehab facility.

I quit my job at the ice cream shop. I can't tell my boss why I am quitting. I can't let her know I've been having methadone delivered to me in between making waffle cones. I hate not giving her my two-week notice, but my mental health needs me. Besides, I believe this job is giving me carpal tunnel syndrome.

CHAPTER 10

REHAB IS FOR DOLLS

I love rehab. I get a tour and feel like I am at an open house. This place is amazing. It's a huge lodge in a secluded place. The teens live in a smaller lodge in the back. They let us smoke cigarettes. *Grab me a pen! Where do I sign?*

"We have five-star food," our guide informs us.

Perfect, I love stars, I think to myself, although the concept of star food is new to me.

I am taken to my room. I have two roommates who do not get along with each other at all. Luckily for them, a future comedian with one stolen act from *SNL* is here. We get another roommate, and now I have a full audience.

Our new roommate's name is Kandice. She wears braces and is one inch taller and one year younger than me. We love each other right away, and I get to feel like a big sister. I introduce her to the other kids, and she tells me her story. She's from a town south of mine and she likes drugs too. When she was little, her mother made her compete in beauty pageants. She won a lot of trophies and had a successful career as her mother's doll, but somewhere something happened, because now she is here with me.

I don't know what happened to me to make me drink and use drugs. The other kids tell stories of how their parents abandoned them or abused them. Some of their parents are divorced. I can't relate. My mother and I fought a lot, but I wouldn't say it was *abuse*. She never gave me a black eye or anything like that, but I am hurt it is so easy for her to keep sending me away. *Why do I always become someone else's problem?*

I do know I can't stand my dad, but I don't know why. He did buy me a carton of Marlboro Reds as a going-away gift. Maybe I am too hard on him. I can't find any reason why I get high. Everyone has a story, but me. "I'm just bored," I tell a counselor.

"There's no such thing as using because you are bored. You are comforting yourself. That's why you drink and use drugs. It's your comfort food. No one taught you how to comfort yourself. There must be a reason you are uncomfortable in your own skin."

We have group all day, every day. I love it. I love talking about myself in front of a group of people. The counselors ask a lot of questions about our parents. I tell everyone my mother controls my life and that's the problem with me. The counselors dig to see if I am hiding anything. Unfortunately, my secret is buried so deep no one can find it.

Our families get to visit us, and then our parents come with us to group. They call this "family week," which we all dread. Our parents take turns sitting in a chair facing us, and we tell them how we feel and how they hurt us. Some of the kids' parents don't show, and they talk to an invisible parent.

Afterward, our parents make lists of all the things they like and love about us.

My parents don't seem to know me at all. My father writes that he "loves the way you walk and talk and your smile" and he "likes when we watch TV together." My mother writes that she "loves that I do what I say I am going to do." *Why aren't they acknowledging how funny I am or how great my outfits are? They don't see me.*

"Ashley, you've been getting phone calls from one of your using buddies," a counselor says, as she approaches me one night. "She says she is your mother, but we know she's not."

"Oh, gosh. That must be Neely."

"We can't let you talk to her. You need to change your friends and the places you go."

"That's fine. I don't want to talk to her."

I feel special I am getting phone calls in here. I am also getting letters from my friends. My childhood friend, Kitty, writes me and tells me she had no idea I was in this place until she called the house and my mom told her. The girls from my high school send me cards. I feel loved. I never want to leave rehab. I learn to play pool. I smoke all the cigarettes and drink all the coffee I want. I have key lime pie every night for dessert, and it is the best key lime pie I've ever had in my whole life!

The counselors care about me. One of the counselors tells me a story about one of his friends. I don't remember the story, but I remember the moral of the story. I bury it in my heart and take it home with me: *Believe nothing that you hear and only half of what you see.*

I leave rehab. Every good thing must eventually come to an end, and inpatient rehab is no different. I like being sober. I like my new friends. I feel there is a hope I didn't have before rehab. I am told to keep going to meetings and get a sponsor. I must commit to my sobriety and work hard at it. This means I need new friends and new places to hang out.

It also means I need to break up with my boyfriend. He does not want to break up. He wants to marry me, and he gives me a ring. I tell him it's over. I want to stay sober, and I can't be sober with him. He has a hard time letting go and calls me, crying a lot. I block his number, tell him he should pursue his career as a fire starter for the Lord, and I move on with my life.

I'm behind in school because I've missed over a month of classes. The principal tells me I will need to repeat senior year. There is no way I am repeating my senior year and graduating with the eleventh graders. The counselors from rehab tell my parents about an alternative school for sober kids. I beg and plead to go there. I need to graduate school this year! I can't do another year of high school.

I enroll at the alternative school. Kandice goes there too. A few of the kids from rehab go, and it feels like we are a family. A few of them get kicked out for fighting or failing their drug tests, but not me. I work hard at staying off drugs. I feel sorry for myself a lot. The other kids know why they have problems, but I don't. *None of my relationships work out. There seems to be something wrong with me. Why do I want to die sometimes? I don't understand.*

"Hey, at least you have your health," one kid says to me.

"Pssh . . . yeah," I reply, completely unaware of the future that lies before me.

I graduate from my sober high school with a 3.8 GPA. It's not hard having a 3.8 GPA in a sober school. After all, we spend most the day talking about our feelings and then spend a couple hours doing algebra. There's no failing sober school; there's only failing yourself.

CHAPTER 11

MICHELOB ULTRAVIOLENCE

Failure looks different for everyone. For most eighteen-year-old girls, failure looks like rejection from a college or a breakup. For me, failure looks like the bottom of a tequila bottle.

I am sober for eighty-nine days before I start drinking again. I don't have a reason or an event that causes me to drink. I just can't see the rest of my life without it. I am only eighteen. I have so many drunks left in me. I'll try again later.

I feel pressure to go to college. I want to be an actress and a writer and so many things, but I don't know where to begin. My mother wants me to go to college. I enroll in a university and decide to major in journalism, but before college comes the trauma.

I spend my summer before college drinking beer and partying. I discover cocaine. I am back to my old ways. I go to a party on an island in the lake with some of my high school friends. I get drunk and black out. Alex the Terrible is at the party. He pulls me aside and tells me to follow him. *He wants to work things out. He misses me.* He tells me to take off my clothes. I don't understand what is happening. I go to speak, but no words come out of my mouth. He pulls my bathing suit down, and he takes from me. I cry.

Another boy is in the woods. Alex shouts at him and tells him to leave. This isn't what was supposed to happen. "Alright, put your clothes on," he says as he gets up and leaves me lying alone in the woods. *Wait, come back. Tell me this didn't happen. Tell me I'm wrong.* I can't move.

The other boy from the woods is now on top of me. "No," I sob.

"Shh, be quiet." I stare at a sock on a tree limb. A tear slides down the side of my face. The boy says something and leaves. I hear approaching footsteps.

"Ashley, GET UP! Everyone is looking for you," Alex shouts at me.

He picks me up and leads me back to the campsite. I fall asleep in a tent with the boy I am dating. I wake up in the morning and I pee. I pee again and again. I can't stop peeing. Everything hurts.

The second boy who raped me is moping and kicking around cans. Everyone laughs at me for peeing so much. The campsite is littered with my toilet paper. I need a doctor. I don't know why I am peeing so much. And then I remember the night before. *I'm a whore.* I feel so ashamed. Somewhere in between the guilt and shame, I bury my pain into the deep recesses of my mind, and I forget it ever happened. The memory is gone, and once again its torment lives on and grows inside me.

PART 4

FORGOTTEN

CHAPTER 12

THE UNTOUCHABLE

Healthy people don't know this, but when you spend your childhood sick, life adapts to you. Adults want to help you. There's always someone who will listen to you cry and wipe your tears. There are treats and perks to being the sick kid. The hard part about being sick isn't the childhood, it's the adulthood.

Suddenly, you must teach yourself to adapt to life. Life is a hard game, and for a sick person, it requires a lot of timeouts. At times, your teammates are busy having fun while you're on the sidelines, icing a broken heart. Some of them wait for you to come back and join the game, and some of them play without you. A big part of having a childhood illness is the adaptation. Some give up and sit out every season for the rest of their lives, and then there are the ones like me. We cannot give up. We take our timeouts, and then we get back into the game. It's about more than winning; it's about being able to play.

College: For some, it's a pathway to success and fortune. For others, it's mostly just debt. For me, it's freedom from my mother and, of course, debt. I have longed for an escape from her castle, and now I finally have it. Unfortunately, it isn't really freedom when your capturer is paying your rent. Freedom is an illusion.

I move into my new college apartment with three roommates. Every night is a party. Life is fun. School is hard, a lot harder than high school. I am stressed out. There is always a paper or essay due. I barely was able to graduate high school. How am I going to manage college? *Easy peasy. Cocaine and meth.*

I am sitting in English class when my favorite professor asks us a question. I raise my hand to answer. Next thing I know, I am on the floor and a handsome EMT is asking me what my phone number is. "I . . . I don't know," I stammer. *I wish I could remember my number. He seems to really want to call me.* I can hardly speak at all.

"You had a seizure. We are going to take you to the hospital. It was a close one. Your face turned blue. You weren't breathing." I look around, and there are all my classmates—including the cutest boy in my class—standing in a circle looking down at me. *How embarrassing.* Later, my professor tells me she thought I was being silly until I started convulsing. Everyone gathered around and prayed for me while she called security.

I have never had a seizure before and do not know what caused it; surely it can't be the drugs. The ER doctors run an MRI and find nothing. They ask me about my sleep, and I tell them I haven't been getting much of it. They tell me I have a concussion and not to sleep, and not to drive for six months. I start walking to class, and the semester flies by.

In class, I learn about comma splices, world wars, and how George Carlin changed legal history with seven dirty words. Outside of class, I learn college boys break hearts as easily as high school boys. My roommate introduces me to her friend, Tom, who has bright blue eyes and a scar across his left cheek. A finance major, Tom also sells large quantities of drugs. For me, he's a small-town Al Capone; he's Tom-the-Con, and he is untouchable by anyone, including me.

It starts as a friendship. I confide in him, and he listens. He's always available, and I am content. One day, he asks me to be his girlfriend. "I got a girl pregnant last summer. I don't want to be with her. I want to be with you. Do you want to be with me?" I think it over, and it doesn't sound like a great plan for me. I'm not ready to be a stepmom. Months later, the baby is born, and she and her mother move in with Tom. He has a family, and I am alone. I miss him.

I text him. He texts me. Sometimes we call each other. I can't let go and neither can he. When his girlfriend, Luanne, goes back to her hometown on the weekends, he picks me up in his 1971 Cadillac DeVille, and we ride around town. Everyone knows Tom and respects him. My life feels like a movie when I am with him.

When I am not with him, Luanne calls me to let me know how happy they are together. She calls me every day. Sometimes she doesn't say anything but just calls and hangs up twenty to thirty times a day. I change my number. She gets my new number from Tom. She loves to torment me. *One day, he will break up with her and we will be together. It's me that he really wants.* I am the other woman with her life on hold, committed to a lie of a future that will never happen. My drinking increases, just like the counselors in rehab said it would if I went "back out."

At home, the girls who live above my apartment stomp loudly, and my roommate gets angry. First, she takes a broom and pokes it onto our ceiling to get them to stop. The girls get mad and stomp louder. We go upstairs and knock on their door. My roommate flings herself into the doorway. I stand in the hallway and watch as she punches one of the girls. They call the police.

My roommate is taken to jail, and I get a citation for drinking underage. It's my second one. I am not sure how I got the first one. I was probably drunk. Two underage drinking citations does not look good. I have my first court case. My mother thinks I am going to jail for a year. I tell her that's highly improbable. She hires me a lawyer. He is a round, balding man in his fifties. As I leave his office, he kisses me on the forehead. I tell my mother, and she laughs, "Oh, Ashley. I am sure you are taking it the wrong way."

The judge orders me eleven months and twenty-nine days probation, community service, and sixty days of intensive outpatient rehab. My conversations with Tom end. He quits returning my texts and answering my calls. He chooses to be a family man, and I choose to move back in with mine. I spend the rest of the semester driving thirty minutes from my mother's castle to campus three days a week, and then I drop out. *I'll get around to college later.*

I meet with my probation officer on Mondays. Her desk is always covered in papers. I don't know why this woman doesn't have some kind of filing system. She looks old enough to know about folders. I sit in front of her. She asks me questions about getting a job and checks my AA paper for signatures.

Once the law gets involved with your drinking, they need autographs of other drunks proving you can show up to a room and listen to a group of more drunks share war stories about what life "used to be like" before they got in trouble with the law or before their wives left or some other horrible thing happened. No one walks into an AA meeting and says, "Hey, I'm new in town, and my life is stable. Thought I would see what y'all got going on in these church basements. Is that coffee?"

While I am on probation, Tom is in jail for violating his probation. He writes me letters and promises one day we will be together. I write him back and tell him I love him. I am no longer the other woman. I am once again a man's pen pal. Our love story is a complicated one written in blue ink from commissary.

In rehab, I do my best to convince the counselors I don't belong there. "Well, if this is your third time here, sounds to me like you are home." *Ugh, I hate these wise guys.*

Rehab with adults is a lot different than with kids. I listen to horror stories of how these adults ruined their whole lives instead of a few years. One man's belly is distended. He has cirrhosis, and he's on a waiting list for his second liver.

"And if I get another one, I'll drink again," he informs our group. *What a jerk. If I ever got sick, I would quit drinking,* I lie to myself.

CHAPTER 13

HOW TO SCAM
A BRIDE

I need a job. Being on probation isn't cheap. I grab a newspaper and look through the help wanted ads, finding an opening for phone sales. *Perfect. I love talking on the phone!* I have an interview, and I get the job.

I call brides at night and tell them they have been "selected" for a free hotel stay, but first they need to come to a conference room in a shady hotel to watch a "cooking show." It's not a cooking show, rather a group of tubby salesmen pitching cookware. If the brides sit through the whole thing, they each get a voucher to stay at a hotel in Bermuda.

We tell them they've been "selected" instead of "won." There are certain words you legally avoid using when you're scamming people. We have a base pay, and we have a very small commission. If we call a bride and she doesn't answer, we leave voicemails. When the brides call back, they say, "Oh, so and so called me. I've been selected to go to Aruba." The call then gets transferred to the girl who called and left the message. If the bride falls for it, the girl gets an extra dollar for the hour. It's very practical, except there's a huge problem. There's already a girl named Ashley at the job.

"Well, we can't have you leaving messages and saying, 'This is Ashley Number Two.' What's your middle name?"

"Brooke."

"Well, there you go. You're Brooke," my manager informs me.

I like the name Brooke. I like being different. There are so many Ashleys in the world. There aren't enough Brookes. Maybe this could be a new beginning for me. Whenever we hire a new girl, she thinks my name is Brooke. There's always a confusion around the office. "Ashley, it's for you. I mean Brooke."

"We're just all gonna call her Brooke."

"Well, I'm gonna call you Ashley Brooke," my new friend, Lucy, tells me.

Lucy is my new best friend. She's a bride scammer too. She is a few years older than me, and she has what I want for myself one day: a little boy, a house, and a boyfriend in jail. She invites me over to her house a lot. She makes me laugh. Whenever her boyfriend calls her, she leaves the room, and when she comes back, she yells, "Ugh, he gets on my last nerve!"

Lucy does not approve of my on-again, off-again romance with Tom-the-Con even though he and her boyfriend have so much in common. I make excuses to her when Tom blows me off. "HOW-EV-ER," she says. She will raise her voice to me like a lawyer in a courtroom disputing my defense of him. She always wins every case with her "HOW-EV-EVERs."

"You need to read this book. It's called *He's Just Not That into You*," she tells me. I don't know what she's talking about. Tom is very much into me. He also happens to be into another woman at the same time. It's complicated.

CHAPTER 14

I'M IN LOVE. GRAB ME A VICODIN.

It's hard being the other woman. Being the other woman is consuming. I'm always waiting by the phone listening for a ring or chime. I'm constantly on edge, paranoid I am going to lose something I don't really have. Being the other woman divides the mind. I am endlessly consumed with the idea that love is almost mine or consumed with the fear that I will be found out and such an opportunity will cease to exist. The other woman never really feels valued. If she did, she wouldn't be the other woman. Being the other woman isn't about love. It's about obsession.

There are times when I am tired of being the other woman. I yearn to be seen. It's times like these I hang out in bars and nightclubs with a giant X on my hands because I am too young to drink, and it's such a time as this that I meet George.

George is at the bar drinking a beer. I am not drinking because I'm only twenty years old. I drank in the car with my rehab friend, Kandice, because I am a responsible future wife. He introduces himself to me, and I stare into his blue eyes and at his biceps. I am listening but not hearing a word he says. I have drifted off into Neverland dreaming of a wedding that will never happen. It's my go-to move. He asks me what I do for fun, and I share with him my dreams of being a writer/actress/comedian. He seems to approve of my interests.

"Hey, wanna be my girlfriend?" he asks me. Now, *that* I hear.

"Yeah, sure. I'm Ashley."

Like so many other twentysomethings, we leave the bar and enter a relationship. He'll look at me sometimes and randomly say to me, "I love you." And he means it. He does love me, and I love him. I can finally tell Tom-the-Con goodbye.

Love hurts. It physically hurts me. Now that I have a man of my own, I am plagued with physical pain. The doctors run tests, and they all come back normal. Something is wrong with me. I see a urologist who begins a trial of medications. Now, I can't go to the bathroom. I am even worse than before I saw him! I am in so much pain. I am admitted into the hospital and given a Foley catheter for a week. Now he wants to look inside my bladder and stretch it, believing this will cure me. He is wrong. The doctors are always wrong. Desperate, I turn to my primary care physician, who refers me to another urologist, Dr. D. She feels confident he can help me, and I trust her.

I am hopeful. My mother drives me to my first visit. We silently sit in the waiting room. There is always a tension between us. "Are you mad at me?" I ask her.

"What? No. Gosh, no," she replies as her mind seems to wander to a distant place. I don't know why, but I sense she isn't being truthful.

Dr. D. becomes my new urologist. He takes his time with me, listening. He gives me what I have been waiting for: an answer. "I am going to start treating you for interstitial cystitis. There is no cure, but we do have some treatments for you that we can try." My chest tightens at the thought of being diagnosed with something that has no cure, but at the same time I feel relieved someone finally knows what is wrong with me. It is the first time I feel heartbreak and relief at the same time.

For the first time in my adult life, I have a boyfriend who genuinely cares about other people. One day while driving home from work, George sees a man's hand hanging out of a car's trunk on the side of the highway. Naturally, he pulls over and opens the trunk. There's a man in there who has been kidnapped. George helps him out of the car and makes the local five o'clock news. *My boyfriend is a hero.* My boyfriend is also my drinking partner.

In August, we take a short vacation to Florida. We drink all night and then in the mornings I make my way to the beach, lie in the sand, and pretend I am in a movie—a movie based on lying in the sand hungover and getting sunburned from mixing sun with antibiotics. I love Florida until I get caught drinking underage again. I don't know what it is with me, but I keep getting in trouble for drinking.

My appetite for destruction is catching up with me. My bladder is not happy. It's getting much worse. I am sure the drinking isn't helping, but even when I am not drinking, there is a problem. Sometimes the pain is so bad, I go to the emergency room. Sometimes I lie on George's bathroom floor and cry, asking God why this is happening to me. I look up at the ceiling, and it's covered with ladybugs. I want to believe the ladybugs are a sign of hope, but I can't let myself be fooled. I am so embarrassed, but George doesn't get impatient with me. He thinks it's going to get better. He is the best boyfriend I have ever had, and if it wasn't for my bladder and his black-out drinking, I would be the happiest girl alive.

When we drink, I pick fights for no reason. I get annoyed with him. He can't hold his liquor anymore, and it's not cute. He blacks out. I hate when he blacks out. Because of my health condition, I cut back on my drinking, but George doesn't. I want a man to be in control, and he is letting me down. My health is spiraling, and I want him to be something he can't be: *my hero.* I am resentful and bitter. I decide it is time to break up with him.

I drive my Honda Accord to his house and wait for him to come home. He pulls up in his Mustang GT with Guns N' Roses's "November Rain" blaring. His pupils are huge. He looks blacked out. He swears he hasn't been drinking, but I don't believe him. I yell at him, "You're drunk! You're always drunk!" I follow him upstairs and continue to yell. Then I throw one of his work boots at him, like the stable twenty-year-old woman I am. I fly out the door and peel out of the driveway. I am done. George doesn't beg for me to come back, and I never see him again.

CHAPTER 15

THEY ALWAYS START WITH THE COKEHEADS

Some women go through a breakup, and they cut their hair. I go through a breakup, and I want to sell cookware. The bride-scamming business is interested in having me join their sales team. Instead of calling the brides and hiding behind a phone, I will be face-to-face with them demonstrating the incredible new line of Pampered Chef cookware and pretend to know my way around a kitchen. This will be my first promotion. The only problem is the sales team carpools together and drives across the South, and I need a toilet every fifteen minutes. I am now going to the bathroom almost twenty times a day.

Dr. D. gets a new nurse, Shelli. Nurse Shelli is so kind to me, and she listens to everything I tell her. She has long blonde hair and bright blue eyes. I love her right away, and I wish she was my mom. She truly wants me to get better. I tell her how I can't stop going to the bathroom and sometimes I can't go at all. It seems to be a problem I've had since childhood, except

I can hardly remember my childhood. I can hardly remember anything at all.

She thinks I will get better one day. "It just may take some time," she tells me. Dr. D. wants me to wear a Foley catheter. He says we need to "give the bladder a break." I feel myself starting to break. I cry and have meltdowns at work. I see the way some of my coworkers look at me. I've looked at women in the psychiatric ward the same way. I quit before they can fire me. I schedule another surgery, and my mother encourages me to get back into school. Sure, I've got problems, but it's nothing a little community college can't fix.

I enroll in a nearby community college. I only need a couple of semesters of classes and then I will have my associate's degree in English. After that, the plan is to enroll in a journalism school, followed by Hollywood.

My childhood neighbor, GT, still lives in my parents' neighborhood. In high school he had a gold tooth, so we called him GT, short for Gold Tooth. He moved into the house across the street when I was about ten or eleven years old. He would ride his bike around the neighborhood every day, and we would take turns egging each other's houses. Now we're older, we've settled our disputes, and we're best friends.

GT and I work together at a factory. His friend's father is the floor manager. We start work at six o'clock, and I spend all day waiting for boxes to come out on a conveyor belt. I take a tool and move it around inside the box. It's an easy gig other than having to be there at six o'clock every day.

GT and I stay up late doing cocaine until one morning I'm lying on the factory floor with a crew of people staring down at me. "We've got an ambulance coming," someone says. "You went down like a tree, hit the conveyor belt, and fell on the floor," the lady who works next to me informs me.

"You look like you quit breathing," someone else tells me. *Another seizure. Great.* I go to the emergency room. The doctor does another MRI. Everything looks normal, per usual. Once again, the doctors tell me I can't drive. They prescribe me seizure medication, and I quit the cocaine for a little while. I can't stand the meds. They make me feel crazy. I feel depressed, and I can't think straight. I am not doing cocaine anymore, so that can't be it. I tell my mother the medicine isn't a good fit for me. She demands I keep taking it anyway and that I need it.

"You're taking the medicine. I don't care what it does," she screams at me. *Whatever. I'm not going to another psychiatric ward.* I stop taking the medicine.

The factory does a layoff, and I am let go. That's how layoffs go—they always start with the cokeheads. I continue college. I am sitting in my new English literature class as my professor does the first roll call. "If I mispronounce your name or if you prefer another name, raise your hand and I'll change it."

She calls my name. *Do I go by the name I have always used and continue to live the life that has been so unfair to me, or . . . do I use the name my old coworkers and naïve brides used to call me?* This could be a new beginning. "Brooke," I reply.

One of the boys I used to party with is in the front row, possibly also regretting some life decisions. "Brooke?" He looks very confused. *Yeah, that's right. I am losing my mind.*

Community college is easy. My theater professor likes me, naturally. After all, I exude drama. She tells me I have a strong voice and casts me to play the narrator in the school's adaptation of *The Vagina Monologues*. Actors take turns delivering their monologues and leaving the stage. My character is the only one who leaves and comes back. My stage presence is the only constant throughout the play, and I love it. She encourages me, telling me the stage comes so naturally to me, and I begin to believe in myself.

"Hi, I'm Jordan," one of the girls from my computer science class says as she stops me. Tall and thin, she has huge blue eyes and long blonde hair. She's wearing pants with "Hooters" written on the side. I haven't made any friends at college and have little intention of making any. Community college is only a pit stop for me. It should be no one's destination. She must have seen me narrate and wants my autograph—my first fan. "What's your name?" she asks.

"Brooke," I reply. It feels like a lie.

"That's cool. Do you wanna hang out sometime?"

"Sure. Why do your pants say, 'Hooters'?" I stupidly ask.

"Oh, I work there. Oh my gosh! You should come work there with me! You would make so much money!"

Being a waitress has always intimidated me. First, I am bad at math, and there seems to be a lot of math involved. Second, I feel uncomfortable talking with people I don't know. I struggle to maintain eye contact. I don't know why it is hard for me to look people in the eyes. It has always been this way.

I had a friend tell me once, "You can't look anyone in the eyes. I can't trust anyone who can't make eye contact." He was a used car salesman. A used car salesman thought I was the shady one. It stung.

Jordan really sells the Hooters thing. "It's so easy, and you can make, like, $300 a night, and all you gotta do is talk to people and take their orders. I love it." I consider it. I need money, and I like easy. I'll run it by my parents and see what they think.

I always run things by my parents. I live my life like a little girl afraid to take the training wheels off her bike, except I am a grown woman, and my training wheels are my parents. It's time to let go of them, but I am too afraid. Sometimes I leave my training wheels behind and ride my big-girl bike like the other girls, but I crash. I hurt myself, and I need to go home. I need mending, and I need my trusty training wheels back until the next time I can venture out on my own.

CHAPTER 16

NO SUCH THING AS A
PERFECT HOOTERS

Living with my parents in my early twenties is as uncomfortable as it was the rest of my life. Nothing has changed. My mother is still hot and cold, figuratively and literally. We fight over the thermostat constantly until my father buys me a window air conditioning unit.

My father is annoying. He's always coming into my bathroom when I am showering. He'll knock on my door and say, "Ashes, I need to take the trash out." It makes me so mad. *Why does he wait until I'm in the shower? He has so many other hours throughout the day he could be the garbage man.* Other times, I will be showering, and he will be sitting in his computer room across the hall. I will hear a knock on my door. "Ashes, I need to pee," he'll plead.

"Ugh, Dad. I am in the shower." *He's so stupid.* And then I feel guilty for being so annoyed with someone who needs to pee—I know how it is when you need to pee. I have a general distaste for my father. I catch myself rolling my eyes every time he speaks. I seethe at the sound of his voice. I don't know why he gets under my skin so badly, but he does. I try so hard to be nice to him, but a part of me hates him. I start locking the bathroom door, and I crank up my stereo so I can't hear his knocking and I can take showers in peace.

"There's a girl at school who says she can get me a job," I tell my parents over dinner.

"Oh, really? Where?" my mother asks.

"It's a restaurant. Hooters." She is silent.

"I was thinking maybe I would go and eat there first and see what it's like."

"I'll go with you," my father offers.

"Okay . . ." It crosses my mind that going to a place called Hooters with my father might be strange, but for some reason, he doesn't really feel like a dad. *Maybe if he supports me, I'll stop hating him so much.*

My father and I get a table. "You want some oysters, Dad?"

"Sure, baby. Whatever you want." Jordan is our server, and she's just as happy at her job like she says she is outside of work.

I introduce her to my dad, and he makes a dad joke. She laughs. "I think you should get a job here, Ashes. I think you'll like it here." I graduate community college, and I start my new job as "Brooke," the heroine of my new life.

I like my new job. I don't like wearing the pantyhose. Even worse, the other girls insist I wear two pairs instead of one. "It just looks better," Jordan tells me.

She's right. Somehow, squeezing myself into two pairs of suntan-colored pantyhose makes my cellulite and dimples magically disappear. It also turns getting dressed for work into a strenuous cardio workout.

Jordan introduces me to all the other girls. She sways when she walks, and some of the other girls fear her. We become good friends, and she tells me she went to rehab for ecstasy when she was in high school too. She's a single mom, and she's dating one of the managers. This is a life I never knew existed.

Hooters is a lot like the show *Cheers*. Employees are always involved in a complicated romance, and the same customers come in every day. Some sit next to each other at the bar, and some sit together at a table. There's a group of guys that come in every day after work and drink and smoke cigarettes together. We call them "Table Ten" because they sit at table ten. Sometimes, I hide under the table and smoke their cigarettes. I also get caught a lot. Much like high school, I find myself in the office regularly.

A guy named Hank sits at one of my tables. He tells me how beautiful I am and how much he wants to take me out. I am not used to men being so direct. I am not really interested, but I still struggle with telling men no, and I give him my phone number. He calls me a lot and annoys me. I don't know how to tell him I'm not interested, so I confide in one of my coworkers about my unfortunate situation.

"Hank? As in Hank Hank?"

"Well, he only introduced himself with one Hank," I explain.

"Oh, you can't date him! That's Shelby's man!"

"Who is Shelby?"

"She's the bartender. She's gonna be *pissed*."

I look at the bar and watch a pretty girl with long red hair throw in an order. Great. I've been here two weeks and already I've made an enemy.

"Hi, Shelby. Umm . . . your boyfriend has been calling me. I just want you to know, I didn't know he had a girlfriend, and I don't want to go out with him."

"Who are you talking about?" she asks me with an angry look.

"Hank."

"Hank? That jerk!" She walks away from the bar, and I watch as she gets her cell phone out and dials a number. "Well, you're not coming up here anymore. She doesn't want to see you, and neither do I!" She flips her phone down. "Well, thanks for telling me. Ugh. He's not even cute. He's got a Charlie Brown head." Together we laugh at Hank's unfortunate head shape.

"What's your name?"

"Brooke." I am committed to this new identity.

"Brooke, I'm Shelby. You smoke?"

"Yeah."

"Let's smoke sometime."

And that's how I meet my new best friend. Shelby is the most popular girl at Hooters, and now by default I am popular too. We go out together after work, drinking and partying. We become inseparable. People tell us we look like sisters, and we both wish we were.

It's fall. For most tipped employees, fall isn't anything special other than a season of experiencing the joy of knowing kids are back in school and will no longer be throwing fries on the floor of their sections.

At Hooters, fall means preparing for "Perfect Hooters." It's the one day of the year when everything must be *perfect*. Corporate comes in and evaluates the store. We take a picture in front of the restaurant, smiling even though some of us are stressed out of our minds trying to live up to the impossible standards of a restaurant that profits off the lust of old men and eighties fashion. Our hair must be *perfect*. Our makeup must be *perfect*. There can be zero runs in our pantyhose, zero stains on our shirts, and zero cuticles. The store must be clean. We spend weeks cleaning the floors and the walls. We even scrape gum from underneath the tables. The fate of our Hooters relies on the success of Perfect Hooters. It's a lot of pressure for a job that doesn't offer a retirement plan.

The day finally arrives, but I'm not doing well. I can't pee. No matter how hard I try to go to the bathroom, I am unsuccessful. My stomach becomes distended. *I do not look perfect.* I look pregnant, and I am not in the pregnant girl uniform. My chest hurts from the panic. I am in trouble. I need to go to a hospital on the biggest day of the entire year. "Shelby, something's wrong. It's my bladder. I can't pee." She looks at my distended belly. "Go to the hospital. I'll tell the managers you got sick." I leave work, and by the grace of God, I do not ruin Perfect Hooters.

CHAPTER 17

ALL WORK AND
NO PLAY

I take weeks off work to return to what Dr. D. and Nurse Shelli call a "baseline." I decide to work for a year instead of enrolling into a university. My job is a constant party. I work, I drink, I smoke, I sleep. Repeat. Sometimes I spend the night with Shelby, and sometimes I stay in a hotel with my on-again, off-again boyfriend, Victor.

My managers nickname me Hotel Motel, and I nickname Victor my half-lover. Half of the time he loves me, and the other half of the time he loves someone else. Victor sells drugs, has children with multiple women, and explains to me the mother of his youngest is a roommate and not a girlfriend. I buy it. I buy every word of it, and I pay him with all my spare time.

I have an unexplainable affinity for fathers who are in relationships with other women. When I am not seeing Victor, I see Tom-the-Con. Sometimes I see other men, but no one stays around. I don't know what a relationship should look like, and I am always the other woman even when I am told I am not. There are a lot of adventures to be had while on the hunt for one's husband.

My sabbatical ends, and it's time for me to go back to college. There is a college forty-five minutes away from work. I can go to school and work on the weekends. It's time I move away and start over. It's also time I stop doing cocaine . . . again.

I hate cocaine. I genuinely do, but it loves me. We've been together since I graduated high school. We're like a married couple, and everyone in our circle whispers and gossips about how badly we need a divorce. I can't sleep most nights. My skin is yellow, and there's a hole in my septum. It's not a good look. I file for divorce. I figure if I can move out of town and throw myself into journalism, I'll have distance from my addiction. I'll have responsibility, another new beginning. Some people quit cocaine and they join a program. I quit cocaine and I get a puppy.

I find Bella at a puppy store. She is a puggle, and I love her immediately. I buy her clothes and shoes. Sometimes it rains, and dogs need shoes. Bella does not like the shoes, and I laugh as she struggles to walk around my new living room.

I have a one-bedroom apartment five miles from campus. I take classes during the week and commute to Hooters on Friday and Saturday nights, and my parents pay my rent. I am working on my bachelor of arts degree and am majoring in broadcast journalism. I want to write for television, and I want to become a director. But I feel behind in life. Most women my age already have their bachelor's degree. They are married and starting families. Some are working on their master's degree. I am potty training my new dog.

When I was little, we had a dog. Her name was Tiffy. We had to get rid of her after she bit me. After that, my mother said, "No more animals." I begged and begged. She let me get a parakeet. I named him Punk. He had a blue mohawk, and he looked like a punk rocker to me, hence the brilliant name. My father would take him outside to "watch the other birdies," as he would say.

One day the wind blew hard, the cage fell, the door opened, and Punk was free. I cried and cried in our backyard. I needed a replacement pet right away.

My mother caved and got me a cat. I would dress the cat up in doll clothes, and she hated me for it. I would walk in the room, and she would run and hide from me. Sometimes I would find her and hold and squeeze her so she could feel my love. I tried to explain my expression of cat affection to my childhood friend, Kitty, at the time. She responded, "No, I have never done that." The cat preferred the easier love of my father.

I convinced my parents to get me another cat victim. I named her Daisy after seeing a picture Drew Barrymore drew of a daisy in a copy of *Seventeen* magazine. I don't understand how people struggle to name their children. It has always come naturally to me.

When I first moved into my new apartment, my mother insisted I bring Daisy with me. I put her in her carrier and brought her to our new home. She was not happy. She cried all the time, and she wouldn't eat. Daisy could not hack college. I took her back to my parents, and my mother said, "Well, we tried."

I love my new puppy. I take her everywhere I can. I have a little pink carrier for her that she won't stay in. On Sundays, we

drive to my parents' house, and she bonds with my father. Like all
my other pets, she prefers his love to mine. Some weekends I stay
with my parents as I work at the restaurant, and Bella bonds even
more with him. When we get back to my apartment, Bella sleeps
in bed with me, and when I am in the bathroom, she sits at my
feet. We are like mother and daughter.

Women plan weddings. Women do not plan abusive
relationships. Maybe this is where I go wrong. I want a husband
for myself and a father figure for Bella so badly that I take the
first childless guy with a neck tattoo. It's a Saturday night, and
I am waiting on a group of guys at table nine. One of the guys
at the end of the table is wearing orange plaid shorts and a
matching orange polo. He has a diamond earring that I am sure
is fake. I flirt with him like I flirt with all my tables. And then I
have a thought: I could bring him home with me, and we could
live together.

At this point in my life, I have never lived with a man. I
have lived only with my parents and a small group of other lost
girls in college, rehab, and hospitals. I have no idea what I am
getting myself into.

Orange Polo tells me we should get together sometime.
He introduces himself as Jack, and I am smitten. He is very
complimentary of me. He tells me how beautiful I am and how
smart I am for being in college. He laughs a lot, and he makes
me laugh. I always love a man who laughs, but just because a
clown makes me laugh doesn't mean I should join the circus.

We spend a lot of time together. I stay at my parents' house
during the weekends so they can watch Bella and I can be with
Jack in between shifts. He introduces me to his family. His
mother's name is Sharon, and I adore her. She has long curly red

hair and beautiful green eyes. She calls me sweetie and invites me over for dinner before I head back to my apartment. His brother, Cane, is paralyzed and always asks me about school and encourages my writing. He also has an older brother, a teenage sister, and an eight-year-old brother whom I adore. I love his family, and I want to be a part of it. It's mostly the love of his family that keeps me trapped for two years.

Three weeks into the relationship, we have our first fight. We are at Cane's house. Jack looks at my phone and sees a text from my previous half-lover, Victor. Jack accuses me of cheating on him. "You're still seeing him? I knew you were a whore."

I tell him he's crazy. Victor and I are over. I just haven't told him about Jack yet. I'll tell him; it's no big deal. Things are moving so fast. I got caught up in our new love and forgot to mass text all my previous suiters. Before I know it, he's dragging me outside the house by my arm, screaming and yelling at me in the front yard. He pushes me down. I struggle to get up. He pushes me down again, and the contents of my purse spill out across the front yard. *What has gotten into him?* I don't understand. I get in my car and drive off to work. Time to clock in.

Jack is sorry. He's Jack-the-Sorry Sack. He texts me and leaves me voicemails explaining his sorrow. He doesn't know what got into him. It will never happen again. He believes this lie, and so do I. Jack is a handful. He gets caught driving without his license and is arrested while I am working. He leaves me a voicemail asking me to bond him out, which I do. This relationship stresses me out, but I am convinced one day it will get easier. Jack only needs to get a job, and then everything will be better. Right now, he doesn't feel like a man because I am the breadwinner in the relationship. Things will change once he gets back to work.

I introduce Jack to my parents, and they smile and act polite. Later my mother tells me, "I don't want you with him. He's trouble."

Meanwhile, Jack warns me, "Your dad wants to fuck you." I feel embarrassed and paranoid. For years, I have noticed the way my father looks at me, and I have hated his sexual harassment. Now someone else can see it, but I know what Jack doesn't, and it's that my father would never act on it.

Sharon lives close to my job. Instead of staying with my parents, some nights I stay at her house, and Jack and I sleep on the pull-out sofa. Sharon splits her time between waiting tables and caring for Jack's brother, Cane, and sometimes we have the house to ourselves.

I am having problems with my bladder—a lot of pain and infections. It is a Saturday night, and I pull up to Sharon's house, grateful to be off work. The pain is so bad, and I hope Jack can comfort me. We get ready for bed, and Jack tells me he wants to have sex. I tell him no. I am in pain. I can't do that. "Then I'll take it," he says to me.

"No, what? No. I said no, Jack." And then he takes from me. I scream and cry, begging him to stop. I spend the night running to the bathroom trying to go to the bathroom and not being able to go. *Did he really do this?*

I am heartbroken. My new boyfriend is not who I think he is, but I love his family, and I haven't had someone commit to me in years. Typically, men are freaked out by my bladder problem. The only men who don't have a problem with it are the men who have other women. I am tired of being alone. I want someone to accept my illness and not leave me. That's all I want. Everything else, I can manage.

"It's time I come live with you," Jack announces. "You don't need to be up there alone. I don't trust it." What he means is he doesn't trust *me*. I have given him no reason not to trust me. We move Jack into my apartment. He shows up with a backpack and an Xbox. "I need a bigger screen than this TV to play my games. We're getting a new TV." By "we," he means me, Ashley. We drive to Best Buy. I open a credit card, and Jack racks it up. I'm bruised and in debt, and we aren't a year into the relationship.

Jack hates Bella. He yells at me, "You love the dog more than you love me." He's insane, and I'm scared. He won't let me sleep with her anymore, and she hides under the bed now that he lives with us. I think I made a mistake. This is not the father I wanted for her.

He plays his Xbox all day while I am in school. He has one job: watch the dog. Jack insists on driving my car. He wants to use it during the day to look for a job. He drops me off at school, and he picks me up. He also has my phone. He needs it so I can call him from school when it's time to pick me up, and he needs it in case a job calls.

It's Thursday, and I am done with class. Jack isn't answering my calls, and I need to get home. Something is wrong. I can feel it. I walk the five miles from campus to my apartment. When I get to the apartment, Jack is panicked. "I tried to save her. I swear I did." *Save who? What is he talking about? Bella?* I run to the bedroom and see my puppy in a box. She looks asleep.

"She's moving! She's fine! She's moving!"

"No, Ashley. She's not. I'm sorry. She got out on me. I think she got hit by a car."

I cry. I cry for days. This is worse than when Punk died.

I need a replacement dog. Jack and I go to a shelter, and we adopt the saddest puppy we see. She is sitting in a puddle of her own pee. I know the feeling. Her name is Pebbles, and I lie as I promise to give her a good home.

Our home is not happy. Jack is incredibly jealous. I come home from school and find him reading my journals. He's read all my precious secrets about Victor and Tom. He screams and shouts at me. And then he grabs a gun. "No, Jack. Please put the gun down," I beg.

"I'll shoot myself. I'll do it. I'll kill myself right now," he threatens.

"No, please don't. I love you," I plead.

He sobs and puts the gun down and collapses in my arms. Poor Jack. No one understands him like I do. He loves me so much, and he's afraid of losing me. If he could get a job, he wouldn't be insecure. Sometimes we love each other, and other times one of us is close to death. Usually, that person is me.

Jack drinks a lot. He gets cocaine and sells it so he can get high. Those are the nights I suffer the worst. Disgusted, I'll be cold to him. He'll get in my face and shout at me. He accuses me of cheating, and sometimes I hit him. There will be a tension in the air, and then his right eye starts to wander. It looks past me instead of at me. Then he laughs, and I know I'm in trouble.

One night, he gets that crazy look in his eye and chases me around the apartment. I run to the bedroom for safety, and then he's on top of me, choking me. I can't breathe. "I can't breathe, Jack. Please, I can't breathe," I gasp. He stays on top of me choking me. I feel myself start to lose consciousness, and then I hear a pounding on the door.

"Police! Open up!" Jack jumps off me. "Get the door and don't say nothing." I open the door to two police officers.

"Ma'am, everything okay?" They scan the room and look at Jack.

"Ma'am, your neighbors called. They said they heard you saying you couldn't breathe."

"I'm fine. Everything is fine," I lie.

"Ma'am," an officer pulls me into my dining room and away from Jack. "I can see the marks around your neck. Everything is not fine. Please let me take him, and he'll never be able to hurt you again."

It sounds easy, but it's not possible. *No one else will want me. I can't let them take him.* "Everything is fine."

The officer shakes his head and walks out the door with the other one behind him. Jack hugs me, relieved he didn't go to jail, and tells me, "I love you. I'm sorry. It won't happen again."

He decides it's time for him to move back home with his mother, and my life becomes harder. Now I have a new expectation. After my classes, I am expected to drive to Sharon's and stay the night with Jack, then drive back early in the morning for class. One night, I wake up to him choking me. Sharon comes into the room to get him off me. He hits her too.

The stress is getting to me. My chest hurts, and I can't catch my breath. My heart feels like it is going to explode. *My God, am I having a heart attack?* I consider calling an ambulance but convince myself I am fine.

I call my mother, who says, "It's a panic attack. You're too stressed out."

She's right. I am stressed out. I have a lot of projects for school, and I am failing film. I am showing up to class with bite marks on my face from Jack's rages. My marriage with cocaine was easier than this, but somehow, I make it through college. I graduate.

After graduation, Jack tells me it is time I quit my job. "It's time you stop being a whore," he explains. I reluctantly agree and quit my job. My mother is not happy with me.

"It's him or us. If you pick him, I'll never help you again."

"Mom, please don't make me do this," I plead with her.

"Who's it gonna be, Ashley?"

"I pick him."

And just like that, my mother is out of my life. She doesn't answer my calls. She doesn't call me on my birthday. Jack and I move into a trailer in a town far away from my parents' house. Our landlord won't let us have a dog. Pebbles stays with Jack's mother now. We don't have any neighbors nearby. No one can hear us fighting. Jack cuts grass for money and takes my car and my phone every day. I spend all my time alone in a house that doesn't feel like a home. This is what Jack always wanted: a prisoner.

CHAPTER 18

FREE BIRD

On a Friday night, Jack really ticks me off—he proposes to me. He was supposed to buy us groceries while I wait for him at Sharon's. Instead, he comes home with a ring. I wanted bread.

"Yes," I say, pretending to be happy.

"Ashley, you can't marry him. Why did you say yes?" pleads his little brother, who has witnessed our fighting.

We both know I can't go through with this. My heart breaks for both of us. "I won't," I promise.

I pray every night. "God, please open a window of opportunity for me to leave, and I will go. Please help me get out of this. I don't want this. Please, God, help me." I wait for weeks for my opportunity.

Jack is stealing my pain medication, he's drinking, he's on cocaine, and at night he still takes from me. "I gotta have it every night," he threatens me. There is no one who can help me. This is a job for only God.

It's the most beautiful day of summer. Jack is drunk and driving my car. He needs a new video game. He takes me into different stores, holding my arm in the air, announcing to all the store clerks his prize. We get back to the car, and he's blacking out. The cherry of his cigarette falls onto my hand and burns me.

"Jack, how about I drive? You're drunk, and you don't have a license. If you get pulled over, you could go to jail. I don't have any bail money." This is my chance. He lets me drive my own car. It's a miracle. I have waited months for this day. We get to his sister's boyfriend's apartment, and Jack starts yelling at me. He's always yelling at me. He also wants a pizza.

"Oh, that sounds great, Jack! You stay here, and I'll go and pick it up for you. Why don't you give me my phone in case I get there and there's a problem?" If you make it sound like you're doing them a favor, abusers will fall for it. I'm almost free. Like Phil Collins, I can feel it in the air tonight.

I get into my car, and his sister runs outside. "Ashley, you gotta leave. He's going to kill you tonight if you go home with him, and there's no one to hear you scream out there." She's sixteen years old, and she knows. She knows the danger I am in.

I pull out of the apartment complex, and I scream, "THANK YOU, GOD!" I pick up Pebbles from Sharon's house. I call my landlord and tell him I'm in danger. He tells me to have the police meet me at the house. I call my mother, and she surprises me and answers her phone. I call my best friend, Shelby. "I need you. I need to move. I'm leaving him."

I give my mother and Shelby my address. They meet me at the house, and my father stays at home as the three of us load up my belongings. Jack has figured out I am not going back to the apartment to get him, so he shows up screaming. He grabs a knife and slices my mattress open. The police show up while we load my things into three cars. I grab the TV.

"You're not taking that!"

"Yes, I am. It's mine. I paid for it."

"It's mine," he shouts, as he slams his fist into the TV. "No one will love you more than me."

Somehow, I doubt him. And suddenly, I am free. Thank you, God. I am as free as a bird.

CHAPTER 19

FOUR-LETTER WORDS

Some domestic violence survivors start new lives for themselves, some go back to their abusers, and some—like me—go back into the life they knew before the violence and live the lie that nothing ever happened.

"You can come live with me, and I'll get you back at Hooters," Shelby tells me. I don't want to go back to Hooters. I want to go into journalism and use my degree. Leaving abuse will do that to a person. You've taken a step forward in your escape, yet you take a step back into the world that was once comfortable. Where there is comfort, there seems to be a sense of safety, whether real or imagined.

Shelby makes room for me in the apartment. I bring my dog Pebbles, my TV, and my new addiction to *The Young and the Restless*. Three months back into my old life, my bladder decides to go on hiatus and I am given another catheter. I take weeks off work because catheter bags are unfortunately considered out of uniform, and I wallow into a state of depression and disappointment.

"It's time you start to learn how to catheterize yourself now," Nurse Shelli explains to me. I am heartbroken. So this is my fate after all. It's not going away. I start drinking again to numb the heartache. This time I carry a small catheter in my purse to the nightclubs in case my body disagrees with how I'm living my life. Shelby stands outside bathroom stalls like my guard, yelling at drunk women rushing me to empty the stall.

I've spent my life reaching for my dreams. It's all I've ever wanted—a career and a husband (with great hair), and here I am with neither. I struggle to achieve what others can do effortlessly, and once I make an achievement, I get knocked down. This last time it was literal. I know God listens to my prayers. If He got me out of that horror movie of a relationship, He can fill my life with purpose too. I pray to Him and ask Him to show me where to go next. I pray He heals me of this awful condition that makes me feel so alone and humiliated.

Shelby and I move into a four-bedroom house. My bedroom becomes my own lair. I lock myself in my room and spend my time playing video games and coming off antidepressants. Desperate to be wanted, I reach out to the most consistently unavailable man in my life, Tom-the-Con. I ask when we can see each other again. "Soon," he says. *Soon* becomes a hurtful four-letter word.

Weed is also a four-letter word—a four-letter word that unexpectedly sends me to prison, my first prison: my parents' house. For six months, Shelby sells weed out of our house. Sometimes she picks it up, and sometimes we get deliveries disguised in huge boxes for children's toys. Our kitchen is filled with giant boxes until my former noncommittal suitor, Victor, comes to buy them.

On a Thursday, Shelby picks up sixty pounds of weed, and on Friday, I receive a call from her while I am with my family. "You gotta come home. We've been robbed. I have someone with a truck and a trailer. We are gonna load up the trailer with your stuff, and you can move back into your mom's. We can't live here anymore."

I get to the house, and my room is untouched. The house looks ransacked, and Shelby is missing one of her Nikes. Not the pair, only the left shoe. It looks personal. She moves across town, and I move back in with my parents. "You should have come home to live with us after *him* anyway," my mother tells me, anxious to remind me that making decisions for myself continues to be a letdown for everyone.

I continue to pray to God and ask Him to show me my purpose in my life as I scratch off "accomplice to a crime" from my bucket list. I search help wanted ads and see the local news station is hiring. I apply. I hear nothing. I call and I email. It's important that a woman pursues her career like she pursues her husband. Make them tell you no, and if they've found someone else, still make them tell you no.

"You have no experience," the hiring manager tells me.

"But I went to school."

"Yes, but you have no work experience in the field."

"Then what's school for?"

"I'm sorry. It's not a good fit."

They told us in school it was important to intern. I ignored them. How could I intern, take my classes, work my job, and fight a man for my life all at the same time? The system is rigged.

Life feels boring again. I am living with my parents, working at Hooters, and still single. It looks like I am never getting out of this castle. It's time Tom rescues me. Tom lives twenty-five miles from my parents' house. We haven't seen each other in years. "Soon" has finally arrived. It's eight o'clock at night. I put on my favorite Lucky Brand perfume, head to the back porch, and await my Prince Charming. Nine o'clock comes, and Tom still hasn't arrived. I call his phone and get his voicemail. "You know what to do. *Beep.*"

"Hi, Tom. It's me. I'm just making sure you're still on your way. Call me back."

Nine-thirty rolls around, and he hasn't called me back. I call again. I try to stay calm, but doubt and fear creep into my mind. *How could I have been so stupid? He lied to me. He's probably with Luanne. Why won't she move on? Their kid is, like, seven years old now. Let it go.* Ten o'clock comes, ten-thirty rolls by. I am getting sent to straight to voicemail, and I am not happy about it.

"Fine, Tom. I don't know why you are ignoring me. I am done. Don't ever call me again." I cry and spend the rest of the evening checking my phone until midnight. I surrender and climb the stairs to my bedroom, collapsing on my bed in tears.

I spend weeks calling Tom. I lied. I'm not done. I want answers. I should move on with my life, but I've never been good at that. I continue working and going to the gym. In between the two, my mind is flooded with thoughts of Tom. I concoct stories in my head of what has happened to him. *Did he die? Would it be better for me if he did?* I keep calling his phone. He finally answers.

"Hello?"

"Hey, Tom? It's me."

"Oh, hey . . ."

"I waited for you all night. Why didn't you come?"

And then Tom tells me the most unbelievable story I have ever heard in my life. "A crazy thing happened on my way to your house. I was getting pulled over, and I panicked because I had a pound of weed in my car. I threw it out the window and flipped my car twice and crashed into a ditch. They had to life-flight me to the hospital. They didn't think I was gonna make it, but Jesus saved me, and I have given my life to Him. Luanne has been here every step of the way and has helped me learn how to walk again. I am going to work this out with her. She's a good woman, and I have wronged her so many times. I need to make this right."

I am speechless for a few seconds. I believe him. I believe every word of it. There's a joy in his voice I have never heard before, a joy I want for myself. "Oh, okay . . . I understand, Tom. Goodbye." My mouth says I understand, but it's a lie.

I live in a world of lies. I lie to myself, and I believe the lies men tell me. For Tom, like so many other people, life goes on. I, on the other hand, live in a constant state of *stuck*. I am always reaching for someone—something—to grab onto and pull me out of this quicksand I call my life.

For years, I believed lies that I would be rescued, and for years, I find myself always grasping and never grabbing onto anything or anyone. If only there was a way for me to live a life of honesty, maybe then I would see my purpose in this world. Where can I be completely honest and appreciated? Who or what would love me if they knew who I really was? Is there a place for a woman like me? Yes, there is. It's called stand-up comedy.

CHAPTER 20

OPEN MIC OF TERROR

The secret to living with abuse is convincing oneself it isn't *that bad.* I lied to myself. I watched movies and read books, comparing myself to other victims I knew, convincing myself our relationships weren't the same. I used words like *complicated* and *hard right now* to describe what I called love.

When I was in it, I couldn't see it. I saw good times interrupted with *hard* times. When I was with Jack-the-Sorry Sack, we didn't have many good times. We had times when he was calm and times when he was scary. Our relationship was a mirror image of my childhood, a childhood I had mostly forgotten.

A pivotal point in our relationship occurred at his brother Cane's house. I expressed my lifelong dream of being on *SNL*, to which Jack responded, "That ain't gonna happen. I'm not living in New York." It was at that moment I finally admitted to myself this man was not going to be in my future. As much as I did not want to be alone, I wanted comedy more. I wanted to be inside people's televisions making them laugh like Chris

Farley, Cheri Oteri, and Adam Sandler had done for me when I was a little girl.

Men came into my life, and I believed we would marry and *then* I could pursue my dreams. I believed I *had* to have a husband to get to where I wanted to be. I spent my life close to my training wheels. I reasoned that when the time came, I would trade out my parents for a husband, and then the road of life wouldn't be so scary. The idea of pursuing a dream by myself seemed unfathomable to me. Ironically, I am drawn to the one career in comedy that thrives off one's solitude: stand-up.

"You should be a comedian," Shelby tells me.

"Well, I don't know about that. Comedians write jokes. I don't know how to write a joke," I explain.

Being a comedian intimidates me. Sure, my friends think I'm funny, and I can easily make the Hooters clientele laugh, but can I make complete strangers laugh? I don't think I can. I want to, but I don't know how. I write poems and sad love letters to guys with girlfriends. Jokes are totally different. They have a point.

"You could totally be a comedian. The bar where I bartend has an open mic night. You're way funnier than those guys," another girl chimes in.

"I wouldn't know how to do that." When peer pressure is applied, I pretend to not understand.

"Sure, you do. Just go up there and be funny. You got this."

Non-comics don't understand that a joke isn't random. It's prepared, written material that's original. It's what the comic has written about their own life or observations.

People tell us, "Put that in your act," as if their thoughts coming out of our mouths to a group of strangers is going to make sense. Some non-comics will insult a comic by giving them a street joke to tell onstage. Few things will discredit a comic more than using a stolen bit or a street joke in their set. Unlike me, an audience can always tell when they are being lied to by someone. Jokes should flow like music with a steady rhythm, but a comic should never be like a musician. Musicians are sexy and egotistical. A comic is humble and clothed. Stand-up comedy is the gritty underdog of entertainment. Only the strong survive. Most of all, it is not Hooters, and that is what scares me the most. Stand-up comedy is uncharted territory.

I sit down in front of my father's computer screen, and I take a risk. I write jokes. Well, not really. I write three pages of a rant about Facebook pokes and challenging strippers to a duel. It's not my best work, but it's something. I memorize it. I want to try it out, but first I would like to watch the other comics and see what this world is like.

I pick up a drunk friend, and I share my material with him. He loves it. I have found my target audience. We get to the bar and grab a table. I order a tequila sunrise. We watch as comics take turns going onstage and telling their jokes. I go to the bathroom. When I return to my seat, he says, "I signed you up! Kill 'em, AB!" Panic crosses my face.

He backpedals, "You don't have to do it. I'll take your name off the list."

I can't back out. When I was a kid, my parents took me to Disney World, and as we stood in line to ride The Twilight Zone Tower of Terror I frightfully watched as the ride took people up in the air and suddenly dropped them. I loved rollercoasters, but sudden drops scared me. The screams of the riders frightened me more. "I can't do it," I announced to my parents. "Can we go?"

As we exited, an older boy looked at me and laughed, "Aww. What? Too scared?" I never backed out of anything again. Spanky's open mic was not my next Tower of Terror. I gotta go up. Like Tom Petty sang, "I won't back down."

I toss back a couple more tequila sunrises. "You nervous?" my friend asks me.

"No, not at all," I lie.

My name is called. The comics clap. *Alright, here goes.* My hands shake, and my voice shakes. I black out. I don't know who to blame more: the fear or the tequila. I hear a couple laughs, then it's over. I remember none of it, but I know I heard laughs. *I gotta do this again.*

"How do you feel, AB? You killed it." *I feel amazing. Are you kidding me? I'll do this a few more times, and I'll be famous.*

I'm addicted. I go up again the next Tuesday. I hear fewer laughs. Reality sets in. This isn't as easy as I thought it would be. I need to write. I need to learn how to write good jokes like the good comics. They have quick punchlines. Everyone laughs. Everyone loves them. I want to be like them, and I want them to like me.

I put myself in training. On Sundays, I sit in front of my father's computer and type out my jokes line for line. I memorize them, and I go onstage. I record myself and then watch the recordings. I listen for the laughs, and if they aren't laughing, I cut it out. I move it. I change it. I *perfect* it.

I read books about comedy by other comics, and I take comedy classes. I need comedy more than the world needs comedy. For years, I have wanted to prove my worth, and now

I have my opportunity. I approach comedy like an abandoned child desperate to be loved and desperate to be seen. In the meantime, I am struggling to sleep at night. I am having nightmares. I dream of a large dark shadow standing at the bottom of my bed, and I wake up with the familiar fear from my childhood. I am convinced something is trying to stop me, but I push onward into comedy nevertheless.

I get booked at a show in Tom-the-Con's town. He and Luanne have broken up once again, and now is my opportunity to show him I am worthy. I call him and invite him. I arrive to the show and immediately regret my decision. I am still a new comic, and inviting the love of my life to watch me perform fills me with anxiety. *This is a mistake.* I get scattered laughs throughout my set and feel unremarkable.

"You did good, boo," Tom encourages me.

"Really?"

"Well, yeah. Of course. A friend of mine is having a get-together after this. Do you want to join me?"

"Sure." *Of course I do. First, I meet his friends, and next, I'll be meeting him at the altar.*

We arrive at his friend's house, and he introduces me to several people. Everyone is drinking and smoking but Tom. He tells me he doesn't cuss anymore either. He seems to be taking his newfound religion seriously, and that's fine with me. I am happy he is single, and I look forward to us beginning a new life together.

I make my way to the bathroom as I overhear one of the guys at his party say, "I like this girl more than the other one." I know they are talking about me. With Tom, there's always another girl. He wanted to see if what we once shared was still there before he moves on forever. I can feel it. After the party, we part ways. I know this will be the last I see of him. I hug him goodbye and cry all the way home.

I make friends, and I lose friends. Comedy is engulfing. It covers every area of a comic's life. There's comedy, and then there's life before it. There is a clear distinction between the two. Before comedy, life is typical. There are friends, social events, relationships, and money. Once comedy enters, all that stops.

It doesn't stop all at once. The before life fades over time, and the friends a comic has for years are slowly replaced with comedians. It's not planned, nor is it done on purpose. It's what happens. It's the nature of it.

At first, it's deceiving. It looks like it's about being funny, but it's more than that—it's about being seen. Being seen gets the gigs, and being seen makes friends. Being seen is what takes a comic from where they are to where they want to be, and not everyone from the before life wants to be in the new comedy picture.

My friends and I drift apart. My rehab friend, Kandice, moves across the country with her boyfriend. My fellow bride scammer, Lucy, moves south with her boyfriend, while my sister, Laura, and her husband move to the beach. Shelby and I drift apart, both chasing love in different directions.

CHAPTER 21

KING OF THE HELL CAMP

Friendship is a beautiful gift from God. I think I need a new boyfriend, but God knows that what I need more is a friend. I look at friendships as chapters in my life. Each one is a segment filled with its own joy and sorrow, all adding revelation to the story. I view my friends as supporting characters in my story. Ironically, it is my role as a supporting actress where I meet my new best friend, Jayme, or as I like to call her, "Yay Jayme," because she ignites the little cheerleader inside me.

I am invited to act in a short film called *Hell Camp* with some other comedians. I haven't acted since community college. I'm overdue. My character is a teenage girl who is murdered while relieving herself in the woods by local serial killer Razorface. I was born for this role.

We are shooting the film at Jayme's house, and our characters are best friends. We shoot our first scene together in her driveway. I have never acted alongside someone, and I am intimidated. As we stand in her driveway pretending to be two dumb teenage girls who are about to experience sudden death, I find myself hoping we can continue this friendship alive.

Jayme has seen my comedy before, and she loves my jokes. She especially enjoys watching me drunkenly fall out of my chair when I think no one is looking. Luckily for her, this is a character trait I will continue to have for years, that and my habit for what she calls "loud whispering." Yay Jayme and I grow very close, and we bond over our faith in God. She becomes my best friend and designated driver.

Jayme has a character she created named Ruby. She wears a giant red wig and transforms. I am in awe. She invites me to play alongside her as her sidekick, Sissy. I've never created a character before, but I put on one of her old wigs, and I become Sissy. Ruby bullies Sissy, and Sissy begs for her approval. She also chases men and cries constantly. I love Sissy. Somehow, I relate to her.

Sketch comedy reminds me of my childhood. I loved playing dress-up and pretending to be someone else. Sketch comedy gives the child in me the opportunity to play. I take stand-up so seriously, but with sketch, I feel like I can let loose. Sharing the spotlight with someone else takes a little of the pressure off myself. I love it, but I feel conflicted. For some reason, I feel like I am cheating on stand-up. *With me, there's always an affair.*

My health takes another turn. I suffer with chronic pain and other health conditions. A nurse asks me, "Are you sure you have never experienced sexual abuse?" *Of course, I am sure.* "I am thinking some of your problems are being brought on by anxiety." This does not make any sense to me. She prescribes me a low-dose anxiety medication, and some of my symptoms improve. Some, but not all. *How will anyone love me?*

I am afraid to sleep. Something happens in my bedroom at night. One night, I am lying in bed asleep. As I roll over on my side, I feel someone watching me. I open my eyes and am face-to-face with a man. He reaches out his finger to touch me. *Dad? Has my dad come into my room to rape me? That doesn't look like Dad. Did someone break into the house?* My mind races in fear. I look down and see the man is without feet. He floats and has a look of anguish on his face. His mouth is downturned. Horrified, I scream. My body shaking, I run downstairs into my father's arms. "Dad, I thought it was you."

He hugs me and kisses me. "You're okay, Ashes." *What is happening in my bedroom? Why did my mind immediately go to my father raping me? My father loves me. This isn't normal. Something is wrong with me.*

The dreams continue. Sometimes, I am outside my body watching myself sleep. I tell myself to wake up, I try to jump back into my body, but my body won't take my spirit. I have another dream I am in a room with a strange woman. A man is with us, and I watch as he heals another man by putting something in his mouth. He sees me watching and looks into my eyes and tells me, "You need healing."

I am filled with excitement. He takes me into an office and tells me he is going to heal my pain and the damage my dad has done from molesting me. I feel sick to my stomach because I know such a thing is not true. He begins to put things on my head. I run from him in fear and wake up.

At night I have nightmares, and during the day I suffer in pain. I continue seeking healing. I am desperate for answers.

I read Louise Hay and Wayne Dyer, who teach me that my health problems can be fixed by thinking happy thoughts. I follow their instructions: I meditate and I manifest my *perfect* health. I fill my bedroom with magical crystals, hoping my problems will disappear into thin air. When my magic act and positive thinking fail me, I blame myself, so I turn to my favorite trick: making alcohol disappear into my mouth.

CHAPTER 22

A DIVE BAR
NAMED DESIRE

I have never made sound decisions while drinking, especially when it comes to love. A new romance serves as a great distraction from my suffering until, of course, intimacy enters the room. It feels good to be wanted by someone. It feels good believing the search for love has finally ended. Relief can come cleverly packaged in the guise of love—that is, until the sender changes his mind.

The first time I meet Stan is at a dive bar outside of town. He's a tall, blonde musician. He also wears glasses and denim shorts, which are a deal breaker for me. I am not interested in Stan, but I enjoy his conversation and sarcasm. We bond over our shared love for performing and eighties rock. He's not just Stan—he's Stan Duran Duran. I introduce him to Yay Jayme, and the three of us spend the summer drinking and playing trivia. Well, Stan and I do. Jayme still must fulfill her role as designated driver.

I sense Stan developing feelings for me, but I have no interest. He's funny and talented, but he's also bitter and cold. He usually sits hunched over a glass of Coors Light angrily watching the room from over the brim of his glass. Some women meet a man, and they know right away he is the one for them. I do not feel that way with Stan. I prefer he endlessly pursue me until I cave, like prey. He's hungry like the wolf.

Drinking with men can be dangerous. Sometimes they assault you, and sometimes they think they love you. One evening after some heavy drinking and eighties trivia, Stan kisses me in the back of a bar. I kiss him back. For some reason, unknown to me, I can never tell a man no. *Do I like him?* "I think it's time we be more than friends. We have fun and get along. It makes sense," he says, presenting his case.

"Yeah, okay. Sure," I agree. *How could a dive bar romance go wrong?*

His love is the kind that grows on me. In the beginning, I feel the excitement of a new relationship. I annoy my friends with the constant reference of his name. At night, he comes to my house, we make out, and we play video games in my bedroom. Our relationship is like all my relationships: immature and aimless. We drink, we laugh, and sometimes we argue. Stan doesn't like to sit with me at trivia anymore. He prefers the loneliness of the bar. He ignores me at times, and I find myself desperate for his attention. Stan calls me one afternoon to end my insecurity and to break my heart.

"Can we go back to the way things were before all *this*?" he asks.

"Are you telling me you want to go back to being *friends*?" I seethe like a fourteen-year-old girl.

"Yes, I think so."

Anger wells up inside of me. I feel like a new car in a dealership and he's the inexperienced car owner. He sees me as shiny and new, takes me out for a test drive, and then decides he would rather walk than drive. Once again, I have been duped.

I have created a pattern. Each time I approach intimacy with a man, I become sick with infections and pain. I become angry, obsessive, and paranoid. I jeopardize my relationships. Rinse and repeat.

I pray God will show me what is wrong with me. I want to move on with my life and I want to be loved, but then something strange happens. I am alone in my bedroom when I have a memory. I remember tents on a campground, and I remember my high school boyfriend, Alex the Terrible, pulling me away from a campsite and into the woods. I see him on top of me, and I hear him yell at someone behind us. I remember him leaving me, and I remember the other boy. I remember staring at a sock and the tear rolling down my cheek. *My God. I was raped. How could I forget such a thing?* And then I remember the morning I woke up next to my boyfriend, recalling the weekend. I remember the shame and the self-loathing. *Oh, that's right. I chose to forget.* I tell my parents.

"Mom, I had a memory. I was raped," I explain.

"Oh, Ashley. I am so sorry to hear that. When?"

"After high school," I respond. She nods her head.

"Dad, I was raped." He stares back at me for a moment. "Uh. Geez, Ashes. I am sorry to hear that."

They don't seem surprised. I understand. I was wild in high school. These things happen to girls like me. "Mom, it wasn't my fault," I explain.

"Well, I know that, Ashley."

Somehow, I don't feel comforted. I do feel hopeful. I have begged God for years to show me what happened to me, and now I know. I can be well now. God has answered my prayers. I should call Tom-the-Con and tell him I have God too. Maybe there is still hope for us as well.

"Hi, Tom," I exclaim, excited he answered my call.

"Oh, hi, Ashley."

"Tom, I found God!"

"Well, that's great, Ashley. I am happy for you, but I can't talk. I am about to walk down the aisle. I'm getting married today."

"Oh, okay," I say, my mouth hanging open. "Congratulations, Tom. I am happy for you," I say, holding back tears.

"Thank you. Bye, Ashley."

And just like that, it's over forever with a short phone call. Over ten years of hanging on to hope for a man who was and never will be mine has ended.

My heart is heavy with disappointment. I feel it is time I let go and move on. It is time for another new beginning. It is time I stop waiting on a man to save me and put that crazy expectation on an entire city. I pack my bags. Chicago, here I come.

CHAPTER 23

DR. SECOND CITY

"Your father loves you so much," my mother cries as my father hangs my curtains in my new studio apartment. "My father never even told me he loved me."

I didn't know my grandfather was so cold to her. I watch as my father steps down from the ladder. My father loves me. I will miss him. My eyes well with tears. We continue decorating my apartment, and they take turns hugging me goodbye.

"It's a new adventure," my mother assures me. She's right. Chicago is a new adventure for me. It's an adventure that starts with classes at The Second City and open mics and ends in misdiagnosed mental illness.

I move to the north side of Chicago in the summer. I love it. My neighborhood is filled with bars that host open mics and shows every night of the week. On the weekends, I walk to the harbor and watch the boats. There's a café at the end of my street, where I can get a coffee and sit outside and watch middle-aged women push their dogs in strollers. I jump from job to job and eventually settle into a comfortable nine-to-five as an administrative assistant. I'm living a new comic's dream.

I begin improv classes at The Second City. Improv could make me a better comic by teaching me to think faster, and it could make me a better actress. I take two improv classes before I realize my savings account cannot commit to the entire pyramid scheme that is improv school. Before I completely drop out, I take a committed character class. I learn that the best comedic characters are the ones based on an exaggeration of our personal flaws, like Sissy who cries out of fear she is going to lose everyone she loves. Of course, I love Sissy. Sissy is more than my character; she is me. Thank you for the self-awareness, Dr. Second City.

I get booked for a show after my first open mic. Getting booked in Chicago isn't much of a problem for me. I perform in bars all throughout the city, sometimes outside the city. I do a couple of showcases at Zanies. I befriend several comics, and I crush on several emotionally unavailable comics. I love every aspect of Chicago comedy.

It's not the comedy that breaks me; it's everything else. I feel rundown most days, even on the days I'm not hungover. I don't have a cold, and I believe I am sleeping well. *Why am I so tired?* I go to a doctor near my neighborhood who insists on running some bloodwork. I call my mother and tell her I am not feeling well. She says, "It's probably allergies, Ashley. You'll be fine. Don't worry about it." As always, the lab work comes back normal.

There is also a psychic school not far from my apartment. On Sundays, they have energy healing classes. *Maybe my energy needs healing. Maybe that'll fix me.* I sit in a chair as women circle me, moving their arms around in slow, dramatic gestures. Sometimes they'll give a person a psychic reading with their healing. I always hope one of them will conjure something up and tell me what the heck is wrong with me, but they never do—a total waste of my ten dollars.

I love going to the psychics. I have my cards read, and I have my palm read. I get my stars read. If there's something that needs to be read, I'm happy to pay a foreign lady in a small store to read it to me. Naturally, my desperation catches up to me, and I am sucked into a toxic relationship with a psychic.

After several months of giving her all my money, an old sock, and some new bedding, my friend Janine intervenes, "What? Why, Ashley?"

"She said it would bring me love," I explain.

"She's a fraud, and she lied to you. We are getting your stuff. Take me with you." I show up to the fortuneteller's shop with my friend behind me, demanding my belongings and my money. She hands me my money and a blanket, looking terrified of Janine the entire time. It's surprising she didn't see any of this coming.

Well, if the psychics can't help me, maybe counseling will. It's time I address this campsite rape anyway; maybe that's why I feel so rundown. Trauma can wear down the body and cause depression and exhaustion—I read that myself, given to me free from Google.

I find a therapist with a private practice in downtown Chicago. "Are you drinking or using any drugs?" she asks me.

"Well, yeah. I'm a comic."

"I won't take on a trauma case unless the client is sober. It won't help if you're drinking." Annoyed, I quit drinking and join a twelve-step program. I commit myself to healing. I meet with my therapist every Wednesday evening, but I have a problem—I'm not sleeping. The other twelve steppers tell me this is normal for a newly sober person, and eventually my brain will figure it out. Months go by, and I only sleep a few hours at night. I feel miserable. My brain is not figuring anything out. I am more tired than I was before sobriety.

"I can't sleep," I cry to my therapist.

"I think it's time you see a psychiatrist. I believe medication would help you." She gives me the number and address of a psychiatrist, and once again, I become someone else's patient.

The psychiatrist prescribes me sleeping medication, and it doesn't help. Convinced I am depressed, she prescribes me antidepressants. They don't help me. In fact, they make me feel worse. Each one makes me feel like I'm strung out on cocaine, but not good cocaine—bad cocaine that's been cut with something awful like Trimspa. I ride the bus paranoid, sleep deprived, sweaty, and with teeth clenched and a heart that feels like it's going to thump out of my chest and into the lap of the guy sitting next to me. I don't know where Paxil came from, but it feels like it's made in a meth lab.

"I can't take this. I feel like I'm losing my mind," I tell my doctor.

"I am diagnosing you with bipolar."

What? How? Bipolar disorder is not on my vision board. She puts me on a mood stabilizer, an anti-anxiety medication, a sleeping pill, and an antipsychotic, and I still don't sleep most nights. *Something is very wrong.*

"Well, at least you're sober," the other twelve steppers tell me. *Yeah, that's what got me into this mess.*

I don't think Chicago could get any worse for me until my boss calls me from her lunch break and says, "Ashley, I am going to have to let you go." She calls me while I am working to fire me.

"You're kidding." *I've never been fired from a job in my life.*

"No, I'm not. Sorry. *It's not working out.*"

Getting fired feels like getting dumped but worse; there are people watching, an audience. I hang up the phone and stare at my computer. *Do I finish my work, or do I walk out the door? How does this work?* And then it hits me. *You leave, Ashley. It's over. All of it. The job. Chicago. Chicago comedy. Over.* Mortified, I grab my purse and head out the door. I'm at a bottom. I call my mother.

"Mom, she fired me."

"She did *what?*"

"She fired me."

"You're kidding."

"No, apparently they don't joke like that up here."

"Ashley, *it's not working out.* You tried. It's time to come home now."

She's right. *It's not working out.* I am not Mary Tyler Moore. I am not going to make it after all. I ventured out alone on my big-girl bike and crashed. Now it's time I go home, put on my training wheels, and hopefully try again another day.

CHAPTER 24

VALLEY OF ASHES

Normally when people lose their jobs, they get depressed, but when you're sober, it doesn't matter. You're already sad—at least I am. I hate sobriety. I don't hate *being* sober. I hate feeling the demonic torment that comes *with* my sobriety. I'm home, but I still cannot sleep at night. I am crippled by anxiety, constantly afraid I won't sleep another night. I am so depressed I can't get out of bed. I lie in bed all day waiting for a sleep that never comes.

I've gained weight from all the medication the Chicago doctor has me on. I look in the mirror and hate what I see. Staying sober isn't hard; I'm too tired to pick up a bottle. The hard thing is believing life will get better.

"You're not bipolar. You're depressed because you've gained all this weight from the medication. I'm taking you off the antipsychotic," my new doctor informs me. "If you can't sleep, go sit in the least comfortable chair you have and read the most boring book you can find."

It sounds easier than it is. Sleep is still not coming for me. I sit on my parents' couch and cry.

"Ashley, stop crying. I'm in my seventies. I can't take care of you now. I must take care of myself," my mother explains to me.

I cry more. I'm a burden on myself and my family. My doctor tells me to keep myself busy during the day so I will wear myself out and sleep at night. I have so much anxiety, I start my day with heart palpitations. The smallest of tasks overwhelms me. I turn to community acupuncture and now I cry in a chair in front of strangers with needles poking out of me.

"Ashes, I think you're having a dark night of the soul. Start praying the rosary," my father tells me. He annoys me. I don't want to pray on beads; I want to sleep.

I'm at the end of my rope, so I do something I haven't done in a very long time—I turn to Jesus. "Jesus, help me. I want to have an intimate relationship with you. I need you," I pray. Two days later, I sleep without one of my sleeping pills. I sleep the next night and the night after that. I'm finally getting some sleep. Something is happening. Hope. Hope is happening!

Life has rerouted me. I expected my journey into comedy to be progressive and like the typical life cycle of a comic: take off to Chicago for an endless amount of stage time, fly into New York to hone my craft, and finally land in an unstoppable career in LA. It does not matter how slow you go; what matters is you don't stop. I, unfortunately, have stopped, and I am stuck in a layover between destruction and accomplishment. It is a painful place to be, and it is a place I will spend many years.

I return to my hometown's comedy scene like a wounded soldier returning home after combat. So much has changed—the faces have changed, the rooms have changed, I have changed. I carry a heavy burden no one can see, but the gratitude I have for being home far outweighs it. The other comics book me and welcome me back. A few ask me what happened in Chicago. Whenever the rare occasion arises, I reply, "Lost my job." This is true. I did lose my job, but to be fair, I also lost my mind a little. After the open mics, I go home to silently battle the powers of darkness.

I am home for three months when, once again, illness returns. Mysteriously, I am exhausted. It is not the typical fatigue I feel from long nights of tossing and turning. This is different. I drag myself throughout training at my job and struggle to drive home. It takes four visits and two rounds of prescribed antibiotics until a nurse at a walk-in clinic announces to me, "Let's test you for mono." *Lord, please let it be mono. Please let there be an answer this time.*

"Yep, it's mono." *Praise God!* This nurse has never seen a happier thirtysomething mono-carrying patient in her life. I accept my diagnosis and spend the next five weeks in bed. I spend the sixth week on the couch. I also spend the entire time scared I am going to lose my new job at a hotel in town. I left Chicago and brought home a new fear: unemployment.

I eventually return to work and struggle to get my strength back. It is hard for me to breathe out of my nose, and I have terrible headaches. I am referred to an ear, nose, and throat (ENT) specialist, and I embark on my new journey of sinus disease.

When I was little, my mother pumped me full of Sudafed. I would say, "Mom, I'm tired. I don't feel good."

"It's sinus. Take the Sudafed." My mother had a pill for everything. Take the blue pill for bladder spasms, take the white pill for infections, take the red pill for sinus, take the green pill for your crazy, and don't forget the Flintstone vitamin. What did mothers do before medication? Love their children?

Medication so easily creates the allure that negligence doesn't exist. To the average person, a child with a handful of pills looks like a mother's worst nightmare, but for some mothers, a medicated child is a badge of honor. "Look at me. I love my daughter. You can tell by how many pills are in her mouth."

A medicated child is a scapegoat, an excuse for every failure a parent has. "If only she wasn't so sick," they'll say, as if the child's illness prohibits the mother from living her life and not her own sociopathy.

As an adult, I am hardwired to run to doctors at the slightest inconvenience of a cough or a pain. Unknowingly, I make them the god of my life. My mother taught me to always follow the doctor's orders, ignore my own intuition, and always trust a stranger with a lab coat. In doing so, I have often found myself to be treated like a lab rat. Doctors prescribe medications and surgeries, make notes of my reactions and lack of progress without much empathy for me, then shove me out the door—not all doctors, of course, but most.

"Well, no wonder you're so tired. You can't breathe. You've got a deviated septum," the ENT tells me as he points to a CAT scan image of my skull. I look at it like a map. I turn my head to the side and nod, pretending I understand while my mind races thinking of all the things I need to do once I leave the office.

"You're going to need surgery. The front desk will schedule you on your way out." *Surgery? We just met. We are moving fast, doc. I like your style.* I schedule the surgery.

A month later, I wake up in the recovery room of the hospital, with blood spurting out of my nose. "Have you been taking fish oil?" a nurse asks me.

"Well, yeah . . . no one told me I couldn't," I reply dazed.

"Yeah, they always forget to mention the fish oil. We gotta take you back to the OR."

Typically, a surgeon provides the patient with a list of all the medications and supplements to avoid. Mine does not. What he does provide me with is two surgery bills. What a great guy! I should bring him home to meet my mother.

After surgery, I routinely spend the year afflicted with sinus infections and eventually another case of mono. My doctor insists it is impossible for me to have mono twice. I tell him I know what mono feels like. *Grab a needle, and I'll grab my checkbook. I'm about to pay you hundreds of dollars to prove you wrong.* The doctor bills pile up. It looks like I will never be able to move out of my parents' home and financially survive, until something happens: love.

CHAPTER 25

I'LL BE BACK

He comes into my life twice. They always do. Men rarely commit to a woman, whether it's loving or leaving her. I don't want it. I don't want Stan Duran Duran's love again. I am bruised and broken. I come with missing parts. For a man to love me, he needs to understand I come *as is*. There are no more returns, exchanges, or refunds. For months, I reject Stan Duran Duran. I won't let him come back. No shoes, no shirt, no service, no exceptions. Like a thief, Stan breaks into my life and steals from me one of the most valuable things a grown woman has: her time.

Thieves are cunning. A thief will convince not only you but everyone around you that he is not a thief, and he is not a threat. You introduce him to your friends, you introduce him to your family, and everyone loves him. He earns a seat at the table. He makes himself comfortable, and then he steals. First, he steals your heart; you believe you are giving it to him, but you're not. Instead, he's setting you up. You build a home for the two of you, and he squats. He stops loving you, he stops paying attention to you, and he starts hurting you. A man's weakness can always be measured by the abundance of his insults. After all, a thief cannot give love; he can only take.

Stan is relentless in his pursuit of me. He goes to great lengths to enter my life again. He sobers up, he finds a church, and he even gets a job. He calls my friends crying, convincing them he deserves another chance. I come home from dates with another man, and Stan sits in my parents' driveway crying in his car. I leave bars to find roses and notes on my windshield.

"You'll never find another man who loves you more than him," my mother says, threatening me with Stan's love. *What if she's right?* I break my own policy and give Stan a second chance.

Our love is immature and childish. Our dates consist of brunch and video games. Two months into our romance and we are back to our old ways. Stan is drinking, and I am on the bathroom floor crying in pain. My bladder does not like my relationship. Honestly, I don't either.

I tell Stan I don't want to be with him anymore. I need help. I need to go back into therapy.

"Ashley, I love you. Let me be here for you," he tells me. He isn't going to let me go. I am too weak to fight him off again. I don't want to be with Stan, but I also don't want to break up with him and lose my only chance at love.

If you deny someone your love and they don't respect your decision, trust that they'll never hear a word you say.

* * *

"There is something we haven't tried yet," the nurse at the pain clinic informs me. "What?" I mutter through tears.

"InterStim. It's a device. It's like a pacemaker. It will stimulate the nerve to your bladder. There may be a disconnect between your brain and a nerve. This will fix that."

"A pacemaker? Like an old lady?" I burst into tears all over again.

"A lot of young women are getting it, and they're having great results. I think it's worth a try." She hands me a pamphlet, and I leave her office feeling defeated. There are no pills that will fix me. Some roads to recovery are bumpy; mine is filled with potholes.

"It'll be cool. You'll be like the Terminator," Stan says, trying to pull me out of my pity party. I read the pamphlet, and I schedule surgery. I have three of these devices installed in me, and each one breaks my heart. I enter each surgery hopeful it will fix me, and in time, each one lets me down. I am at war with my health; my bladder and my sinuses have allied against me, and I lose every battle.

My mother complains I am running up her water bill with my frequent trips to the bathroom. My weeks are filled with doctor and therapy appointments. I do my best not to cry at my appointments. If you cry, they'll label you histrionic and blame your symptoms on your emotional distress. I save my tears for the morning commute to work. Sometimes I cry at work and my coworkers look at me with pity. I feel humiliated and alone. I can't find the funny in any of it.

"Ashley, it might be psychological. We need to get into your subconscious," Nurse Shelli suggests. *There's no way. It can't be in my head. I would know if it was all in my head.* "I want to introduce you to Lindsey. She runs a clinic that helps patients like you."

I meet Lindsey, and she and her team introduce me to mindfulness. I return to trauma therapy. If it's all in my head, I want to get it out.

I am now having some good days. They are random. I cannot pinpoint what is helping me the most. Is it my diet? Is it the InterStim? Is it mindfulness? Is it therapy? There seems to be some change. I am grateful. I journal my symptoms. I notice whenever I tell my mother I am having a good day, my symptoms reemerge. I can't imagine how there could be a link. I reason it must be a coincidence.

Living with my parents is getting harder. My father is always across the hall on his computer while I hide in my room. I never fully feel privacy. They are both retired and spend their evenings yelling at the news. *How can I become well in this house? How can peace survive in a household of chaos?*

As I am cleaning clothes one morning, I notice my dog, Pebbles, isn't around. "Mom, have you seen Pebbles?" I ask.

"Ashley, Pebbles ran out into the interstate and got hit by a car this morning." My stomach drops. I feel myself go pale. My eyes well up with tears and then she laughs, "Jesus, Ashley. I'm kidding! If Pebbles died, it'd be the first thing I said to you this morning. You don't think I would wake you up to tell you your dog died? Come on. What kind of mother do you think I am?" Oh, I don't know. The serial-killing kind?

It's time I move, but first I must convince Stan it's time he moves out of his parents' house too. I can't be the only adult in the relationship . . . that would be a felony. I move into our new place first. Stan joins me two weeks later with a backpack and a toothbrush.

"I don't want to have a set bedtime," he tells me. He approaches our new commitment like a kid on a camping trip. I have been promoted from girlfriend to den mother.

I am having problems breathing again. I don't know that they ever really went away. I am sent to another ENT, who informs me I still have a deviated septum. I have no idea what the first surgeon did other than give me debt and a fear of omega-3s. The second ENT insists he can help me, but he doesn't. He only helps me meet another deductible. I am finally sent to a plastic surgeon, who does more for me than the other two doctors combined. He helps me so much, I plan on becoming a repeat customer. I will visit him in another ten years for my facelift.

It's hard having a relationship and health problems. I feel like a burden to Stan. He is here for me, and most importantly, he doesn't leave me. He gets angry, and I blame myself. I know it is hard to be with me. I cry a lot, and there's always a surgery waiting in the wings. No one signs up for this—well, actually he did. I gave him a get-out-of-jail-free card, and he didn't want it. I knew it would get ugly, but he wanted to be a hero. Heroes save lives, not sick girlfriends. Heroes also don't drink on the job.

Twelve-step programs have this saying, "Sick and tired of being sick and tired." This is where I am—sick and tired of being sick and tired. I am also sick and tired of running from doctor to doctor. None of it makes sense. I am sick with one thing, so I have a surgery. Another part of my body shuts down, and I either have another surgery or no one has any answers. After that, I catch a virus. What I need to catch now is a break.

CHAPTER 26

EXORCISE HER?
I HARDLY KNOW HER.

Something odd is happening in our home. There's a heaviness around me. There is a darkness I can feel. I am afraid, and it reminds me of my childhood. I don't recall my childhood, but I know I was very afraid. I have terrible nightmares. Sometimes Stan holds me until I fall back asleep. When he's out late with his friends, I leave the light on in the hallway. I can't be in the dark. I am terrified, so I pray.

I have always been a woman who prays when things are bad. I haven't always been a woman who prays when things are good, which is my bad. I'm working on it. I grab an old Bible my mother gave me when I was in high school. I bring it into my new home, and I read while listening to worship music. I write down my prayers to Jesus, asking Him to help me and to show me why I am so afraid, to heal me. *He healed so many people in His book. Why won't He heal me too?* I am living on a prayer, and I need a new hero. Mine's drunk again.

I tell my father about the darkness in our home. He gives me books about spiritual warfare and deliverance. *Why has he never told me about this stuff?* I learn about the battles between good and evil. I realize not everyone can feel what I feel. Not everyone sees the darkness crouching in corners of rooms like I do. I read about sin and the demonic and how our sin welcomes demons into our lives to torment us, like making us sick and giving us nightmares. *Uh-oh. Someone needs a priest. She is me. I need a priest.* I call my sister. She's a practicing Catholic; she'll know where I can find a good one.

"Laura, I need a priest. Something strange is happening. Dad gave me all these books about people who have demons, and I think I have a demon."

"Dad? Dad gave you books like that?"

"Yeah, I thought it was weird too."

"Yeah, he acts so much holier than thou. I always wonder if it's guilt from the affair."

"What affair?"

"Oh, you didn't know? Dad had an affair for six years. Her name was Myrtle. Mom got pregnant with you during it. Mom and Dad were not the only ones surprised to find out she was pregnant," she laughs.

"What? Dad had an affair?" I'm shocked. *Who is he?*

"Yes, Dad had an affair. I am sorry to hear about all of this. There's a priest near you who is supposed to be a healer. He can probably help you."

I hang up the phone in shock. I had no idea. *Did I ever know about this? Why didn't anyone tell me about this?* Dad has always been so annoyingly religious. I would never think he was an adulterer. *What else don't I know?*

I find the priest's church and go to Mass every Sunday. I ask him for a meeting, and I confess my sins. I tell him about my sicknesses, my sleepless nights, the darkness around me, and my fear. He says a prayer over me and tells me I will be better soon. Weeks go by, and I am not better. Desperate, I run back to his office. He leaves and comes back with a small black bag containing a sash, which he puts it on. I watch as he pulls out a Bible, some holy water, and a crucifix. He prays exorcism prayers over me. Nothing happens. My head doesn't spin once.

I continue to reach out to the priest. He tells me I am choosing to live in sin by living with my boyfriend outside of marriage. I feel so much guilt. I believe there is something wrong with me, and to fix it, I need to stop having premarital sex. After all, sex is hurting me. I don't want to tell Stan this. I don't want to pull this aspect out of our relationship, but I also want to be healthy. I tell him, "I want us to wait until we are married, Stan. I am having too many problems. I think God wants me to wait." Stan is not happy, but then again, he isn't that happy anyway.

"What about my needs? I've been more than patient with you," he tells me. *He has a point. He has needs, and he doesn't leave me. I owe him.*

"It's a simple fix. He could just marry you," the priest informs me when I return to his office, once again in despair. I haven't been having sex with Stan, and I still feel sick. I have so much guilt and fear. "Some people suffer more than others, and it is okay. God allows it. I have someone who is going to help you. His name is Jansen. You will start meeting with him on Wednesday here in the church office."

CHAPTER 27

THE MAN WITH THE
MASTER PLAN

When you spend most your life surrounded by darkness, you forget what light is. That is what happens to me. With every heartbreak, every betrayal, and every lie, the light around me dims more and more. It isn't something that happens suddenly. Losing the light happens gradually, like a curtain slowly being drawn at the end of a play. To me, it appears the curtain has finally closed, but to God it is merely the end of act 1. The lights are coming back on. The story is only getting started.

I return to the church the following Wednesday and meet Jansen. I am surprised to find out Jansen is not an exorcist. He's not a priest or a deacon at all. Instead, he's a regular guy with a wife and kids. Jansen has a gentleness and kindness to him unlike other men in my life. It catches me off guard. He seems so peaceful. He speaks slowly and retains a smile through each sentence that rolls off his tongue. Whatever he has, I want it and I want Stan Duran Duran to have it too.

"We'll start with Matthew 18," Jansen informs me. Matthew 18 tells a parable of a master and his servant.[5] The master forgives the servant of his debt; however, the servant refuses to forgive his own servant. His lack of forgiveness angers the master. The master hands the servant over to torturers.

"Do you understand this parable?" Jansen asks me.

"Maybe," I lie.

"You see, God forgives us. The debt has been paid. But when we don't forgive others, we are handed off to the torturers. In our case the torturers are the demonic. Do you understand?"

"Oh, yes. I understand that," I reply.

"Good. Next, we'll start your deliverance counseling."

I don't see myself as having a problem with forgiving or being angry. This sounds more like something my mother needs, but I'll try anything to have a normal life. I meet with Jansen and two other women in that church office for six months. I struggle daily with my health. My bladder is crippling me. The InterStim is failing me, I contract another mysterious virus, and I become so sick I take short-term disability from my job at the hotel. I lose sleep, and I cancel shows. There are many weeks when I cannot meet with Jansen and the two women, and I find myself impatient, but I learn to trust God's timing.

One day, I am at a Goodwill store looking for a baby book for a friend. Out of the corner of my eye, I see my name on a picture. I turn my head to see if I am mistaken . . . I am not. There is a picture frame with the words, "Ashley, Trust Me. I Have Everything Under Control. —Jesus." I sob. And yes, I buy the picture. *I am going to make it after all, just like Mary Tyler Moore.*

In that church office, I forgive my father for not being a better dad. I don't know what it is that he has done that makes me hate him so much, but I choose to forgive him. I forgive my mother for controlling my life and fighting me so much. I forgive old boyfriends, the boys who raped me, and myself. I decide I want to give my life to the Lord; this means I need to change. I need to clean up my act and get rid of the dirty jokes. It is also time I commit to waiting for marriage. I feel lighter with each session. I also feel happier despite my suffering. I am being delivered from the hands of the enemy and deeper into the palm of God.

I feel the change happening. Jansen prays with me in that little church office, and something amazing happens. The room brightens, and I am struck with the realization that I have been living behind a veil of darkness. Now the veil is torn, and I can see the light of the world around me. The demons flee, and I hear a beautiful voice. It has a sweetness to it, but it speaks with such authority. The voice of the Lord tells me, "You will do so many things."

CHAPTER 28

LITTLE MISS GOODY TWO-SHOES

In high school I assumed the other kids had it easier than I did. There was something about their lives and their demeanors that led me to believe they had something I did not have. I figured it was because their parents were rich.

I was probably right, but now looking back I can see it wasn't only money they had—it was Jesus. Some of the girls invited me to their churches and were trying to get me saved. As a Catholic, I didn't understand this concept of being "saved." Catholics don't need saving. We need priests and wine.

I thought some of them were nerds or goody two-shoes. I would sit in my Bible class and play devil's advocate with our teacher. I didn't want anyone to believe there was anything available to us but suffering. At the time, I did not know why I would do such a thing. Now I can see I was a hurt little girl, and hurt little girls hurt others. Then some of us grow up and make art out of our pain.

I want to believe being a Christian will make my life easy. I want to believe now that the demons are gone, everything will quickly fall into place. I toss out all my dirty material and believe that soon the Lord will bless these loose fifteen minutes, and I will sell out theaters with it. I am mistaken and possibly delusional. Then again, delusions make for great comedy.

Life is better, but it is not easier. It comes with some challenges, but I do feel a weight come off me. I no longer need to manifest and attract people, places, and things into my life. I can let God do the heavy lifting. Besides, all that manifesting and attracting never worked out for me anyway. If it did, I wouldn't be a sick waitress working in a hotel. I would be a healthy comic living out of hotels. I also would have a ring on my finger and a savings account. I throw out my vision board and eventually the failed relationship I have spent years manifesting into a blissful marriage.

The more time you give some people, the slower they move. For years, I have wanted to marry Stan Duran Duran, and for years, he has given me excuses. At first it was that we couldn't financially make it. Then we couldn't get married because I was always sick. Now, we can't get married because he hates the Catholic Church. Having all my friends get married while I am nagging my boyfriend to marry me humiliates me, but I joke about it onstage and tell audiences he took me out to dinner for our anniversary—he got a steak, and I got another day without an engagement ring. They laugh and I lie to myself that he only needs a little more time.

I am convicted to commit to celibacy. I know God is going to heal me, and I know He wants me to stop having sex outside of marriage. I know the two are connected, and I'm no doctor, but I am guessing being raped by my friend and my ex-boyfriends has something to do with it. I think it's Stan who needs time, but it's not . . . it's me. I need time to heal.

Stan Duran Duran is no longer the compassionate person he was when he pursued me. He tells me I have betrayed him. I explain to him the violence in my life, and the conviction and the hope in my heart for healing. He does not agree. He yells at me in fits of rage, "Your problem is that you aren't dealing with your sexual trauma!"

We have different definitions for the word *betrayal*. He punishes me as he withholds his love from me. He moves away from me when I kiss him, and he laughs at me as he yanks his hand from me when I hold it. I miss the old Stan. Stan's love is now as harsh as my mother's. The more he breaks my heart, the more I want to break our lease.

On a Friday, I start a fast. I have never fasted before other than quitting chocolate for Lent. You're not a Catholic woman until you've quit chocolate for Lent. It's in the fine print. Fasting is new territory for me, and I believe it will help me. I have a knowing inside of me. On Saturday, I make it two hours without having to go to the bathroom. My InterStim is turned off. I am on zero medication. This has never happened. *Am I experiencing a miracle? Could this really be happening?* I keep it to myself and thank God for his mercy. Sunday, my symptoms come back. I do my best not to think about it. I continue to thank God for a good Saturday. *I have good days and bad days until eventually there are no more bad days.*

For the first time in my life, I am not chained to the toilet. I can work like everyone else. I don't have to search for a bathroom every time I arrive somewhere. There are some nights at work when I don't even think about going to the bathroom. It is a miracle. God is moving in my life. It's finally happening! I am healing!

Excited, I tell Stan. "It's a miracle. God is healing me."

"God is not healing you. You haven't eaten in a few days. Your body chemistry has just changed. You should see a nutritionist."

A nutritionist? I am experiencing a miracle, not high blood pressure. I want to break up with him. *This is not the one.* I don't let Stan take this from me. I tell all my friends and all my coworkers what God has done for me. I tell some of my religious friends at work that Stan doubts me. "Stay with him. This is how he will know God," one of my coworkers says.

One night, I come home from work. Stan is sitting on the couch. His mood is gentle. He has been waiting for me to come home. This isn't like him. He has something to tell me. I don't think I am going to like it.

"Everything okay?" I ask.

"Sit down," he pats the couch next to him. *Please, God. Don't let him propose.*

"I have some bad news. Pebbles died."

I am shocked and speechless. I expected him to propose, but now he is telling me my dog has died. This is the second time in my life I feel heartbreak and relief at the same time. I cry and Stan holds me. He knows when he's supposed to be a good guy. He, like my mother, is a great pretender.

CHAPTER 29

BUT I BROKE UP
WITH COCAINE

I'm not feeling well again. Rundown and plagued with migraines, I visit my primary care doctor. After my second or third visit, he suggests something I have never considered: "Could it be dread?"

Dread? No, I'm sick. I leave his office insulted, and then I contemplate. *Could dread feel like illness? Could he be onto something?* I think of the nights I enjoy to myself while Stan works and how I dread his coming home. I dread being stonewalled, and I dread the fighting. *Could the dread be making me sick?*

Shortly after my doctor's visit, I am on my way to work when I pull off the highway and approach a red light. I am hit with a strong sense of déjà vu. It lasts longer than typical déjà vu. I question my time traveling abilities. I continue to the hotel and park my car. I clock into work and start my shift. As I approach a man at one of my tables, I experience tunnel vision, and I feel lightheaded. He seems close and far away at the same time. Something isn't right.

"Are you okay?" the bartender asks me.

"I don't know. I feel weird."

Someone gets my manager, and I am made to sit down in the hallway behind the restaurant. EMTs from the hotel come to check on me. They look into my eyes and check my vitals. "Ma'am, you've had a petit mal seizure." *A seizure? Again? How? I broke up with cocaine.*

"You're going to need to see a neurologist. Do you have anyone who can drive you?" *Stan. Stan can drive me.*

"You look fine to me. Do you think you need to go to a hospital?" Stan asks.

"No, I'll just set up an appointment with a neurologist. I'll be fine."

In the car, I call Yay Jayme to tell her what has happened, and I stumble throughout my sentences like a woman who's just had a seizure.

"Put Stan on the phone right now." I can hear her yelling at Stan, demanding he take me to a hospital. I insist I am fine, and we head home.

"Ashley, I have tickets to see Bon Jovi tonight. Is it okay if I go, or do you need me to stay home with you?"

Of all the days you could perform here, Jon. "You go. I'll be fine." *I always am.*

I see a neurologist shortly thereafter. Because of my InterStim, I am unable to have an MRI. I don't mind; that's another bill I don't want to pay. Besides, they can never find anything wrong with me. I tell the doctor about my migraines.

"Are you stressed?" she asks me. I think of my job, and I think of my relationship. Yes, I am stressed. I spend my evenings running around pouring wine for rich people, and then I come home to a whiny boyfriend. It's more than stress. *I am trapped.*

Stan goes shopping at Best Buy and buys a big-screen TV. I come home and see my small old Samsung sitting on the floor of the dining room. I watch as Stan's new TV stares back into his eyes, like two star-crossed lovers.

Our apartment feels different. The energy of the room feels as if it has shifted. It strangely feels happier. I walk over into the dining room and look at that old TV at my feet. There's a heaviness about it. It's small, but it looks like it weighs one hundred pounds. It was with me at my parents' house, it was with me in Chicago, it was with me at Shelby's, and it was trapped with me with Jack-the-Sorry Sack. I see the smear across it from where he hit it. For the first time since I packed up and left him, I remember him punching it and yelling at me, "No one will love you more than me."

I look at Stan as he holds his PlayStation remote with a smile on his face. *It's the same thing. It's the same relationship, it only looks different. I need out. It's time I am set free. And I need to get rid of this TV.*

"It's not working out," I break the news to Stan. "You can move home with your parents now and sign the lease over to me."

At first, Stan pushes back. He retaliates and buys me a ring I don't want. He tells the lie of how I stole and broke his heart. And just like old Stan, he shows up where I don't want him, and he sends me gifts I don't want. He's back to his old ways, but it's too late. I no longer need him to be a hero. I am no longer stuck in my mother's castle. *I have been saved.*

CHAPTER 30

ONE COPAY AT A TIME

It's easy to leave a relationship and blame the other person for its failure and demise. It's easy to harden the heart and let bitterness take root, prohibiting any chance of growth and maturation. What's hard is planting a new tree and watering it regularly with love and compassion. What's even harder is waiting for it to slowly grow, mature, and bloom into a tree of righteousness.

After leaving Stan Duran Duran, I plant myself directly onto my therapist, Carrie's, couch. This isn't the type of relationship a woman can leave and act like it didn't happen. This was more than falling off a bicycle. It was more like a motorcycle crash where I have been thrown onto the pavement of a cold, hard reality—*I have been abused.*

The entire relationship deceived me. Obsession presented itself as love, and I fell for it. It quickly turned on me, and I wasted years forcing it into a healthy place it could never be. He hurled insults at me and convinced me I couldn't survive without him. I believed the lies he sold me, and I quit believing in myself.

He wasn't the only one who let me down. *I* let me down. I once again made the nearly fatal mistake of confusing a man for a job. I worked hard on that man. Each day, I came to work. I clocked in and became his manager. I tried to manage his drinking, his spirituality, and the way he loved me, and like a disgruntled employee, he harbored resentment toward me and created a hostile work environment. I needed to let him go long before I did, but I couldn't bring myself to do it. There were times I threatened to fire him, but he would fire back, "You're too sick. You can't make it financially without me." I believed him—that I would fail without him—but I was wrong. Now that Stan is gone, my stock value shoots up.

After wasting years of trying to resuscitate a dead relationship, I am ready to begin a new life for myself. My health has always been a struggle, especially since my return home from Chicago. I have gone to doctors and had surgeries, but I also go to therapy. With Carrie's help, I make accomplishments, and then I move on. I believe my health problems and my psyche are linked. I refuse to give up on healing my mind and body. Each time an issue presents itself in my life, I gladly pay my therapist to help me get through it. Yes, there were times when Carrie questioned my relationship. Everyone around me questioned my relationship. I couldn't see it for what it was until I decided to take control over my own life instead of trying to change his.

I begin my journey of taking ownership of my emotions. For years, I blamed Stan Duran Duran for my distress, and before him, I blamed other men for why I was angry, sad, or disappointed. I grew up in a household where my feelings weren't allowed. I was taught if I did feel anger or sadness, I had to stuff it down. I had to be *perfect*. If I ever exhibited a loss of emotional control, I couldn't admit they were my feelings. There would be a counterattack. I would be blamed for being irrational and *wild*. Someone had to be blamed for my negative disposition. Being teased at school served a purpose. I could easily blame the boys or my teachers for why I was inconsolable at times. I could never let on that I was just a sad little girl for reasons she did not understand.

Unfortunately, breaking up with abusers is never an easy break. They don't like to let go. Their fear of abandonment causes them to use war tactics such as gaslighting, control, humiliation, smear campaigns, and violence to keep their victims with them. Healthy people don't stay in these types of relationships, and that's my problem. I'm not healthy.

Sadly, after our breakup, my bladder is no longer healthy either. The emotional distress of fighting for my freedom from a warden who refused to let go sets my body back to where it was before I met the Lord. I feel disheartened and heartbroken, once again.

Carrie and I entertain the idea that being ill could be a defense mechanism learned in childhood. Life gets hard, and I check out and check in to a doctor's office, hospital, or rehab. *Could my subconscious be making me sick whenever I feel afraid or frightened? Is there a part of me that is afraid of success and is keeping me in arrested development? Did being sick ever serve me as a little girl locked in her room? Was there a time in my life when being ill kept me safe?* Anything is possible.

I fill up her calendar with appointments, and we tackle each speculation one copay at a time. I am determined to get answers, and like always, I never give up that tiny thing called hope. In the meantime, I confront my father about his former mistress, Myrtle. "Dad, I know about Myrtle. Did you love her?"

He stares back at me, shocked. "Well, that was a long time ago," he tells me, as if the distance of time could negate his feelings for a woman. I can tell by the look in his eyes that my questions have stirred a curiosity in him. *I would love to meet the woman my father pretends he has forgotten.*

CHAPTER 31

DAD'S GOT MAIL

Disappointment can be a comedian's lifeline. Comedians rely on being relatable, and what is more relatable than the disappointment of a failed relationship? I can't be the only woman who supervised her boyfriend. I delve into comedy and tell jokes about how my codependent nature has failed me and my biological clock. It's hard to meet a hormonal deadline when your boyfriend won't show up to the job.

I doubt I will ever have a relationship as long as my parents' fifty-three-year marriage. After all, it's hard to split up when your kid is always in rehab. I start a YouTube channel and create characters based off women I wait on at the hotel or other women I have befriended in my lifetime. I've lost years in a loveless relationship, and now I thrive off likes and comments from strangers behind keyboards. I'm back to my high-school internet ways.

Once again, I sit behind my father's computer printing out some paperwork when I see he has left his email open. He does this often, and typically I close it, but this time I see something out of the corner of my eye that catches my attention—Myrtle's name. He's been emailing her. *This is my fault. I shouldn't have brought her up. He went looking for her.*

Once again, I find myself awkwardly confronting my father. "Dad, I found your emails with Myrtle."

"You weren't supposed to see that," he replies, shocked. He doesn't sound angry with me, rather more like a criminal who is relieved to have been caught.

Once again, I am an accomplice to a crime. "Dad, you can't do this. Mom will kill you if she reads these," I explain.

"Okay, I'll stop," he says, lying to me. *I know to believe nothing that I hear and only half of what I see*, but I believe my father for some reason. Oh, that's right—delusion.

I discover my mother is angry with me for the demise of my relationship with Stan even though she never wanted me to leave her house, which is news to me. Usually, parents are ready to push their children out the door. "It's your own fault. You should never have left here to shack up with him," she shouts at me. Oddly, she also wanted me to stay with Stan. She wanted me to stick it out, save my money, and move out on my own when the lease was over. I think she wanted me to wait until I changed my mind about leaving him.

She's mad at me for leaving her, and she's mad at me for leaving Stan. She's mad at me for thinking for myself. I turn to my father for some validation. "Ashes, don't think about it," he tells me. This is some of the unhealthiest advice I have received from him. It's right up there with his favorite anecdote, "Never trust a man who doesn't drink," as if it's the men who can control their appetites that are the danger. My father doesn't have a clue. If my mother wasn't making decisions for him, too, I don't know how long he would have lasted in the world.

I begin to stick up for myself with my mother. It's something I haven't done since my high school rebellion. I answer less and less of her calls, and I cut back on visiting her. I refuse to be punished for making decisions for my future; however, once my lease is up, I move into an apartment two miles from her house. My boundaries are incredibly skewed.

My father and my friends help me move, and my mother shows up. She looks high as a kite on her pain medication, and I feel embarrassed in front of my friends. She sits at my kitchen table with her nose in the air and insults my décor. She makes snide comments about my dying plants. Yes, my plants are dying, and I refuse to give up on them. We've been through so much together, and I have overwatered them to overcompensate for the days I forgot about them.

I love my new apartment. I am on my own again, and it feels great—I feel free. As I heal from codependency and perfectionism, I continue working with Carrie. As I do so, I learn my relationship with my mother has set a standard for toxic relationships. I make some major strides. For one, I begin making decisions for myself and not for my mother's approval. I even allow myself to make mistakes. I stop beating myself up, and I become financially independent. Sadly, my health is still a problem, but I feel as if I am closer to the finish line. Eventually, I hope to sprint forward into the life I've always wanted.

CHAPTER 32

TORNADOS AND PANDEMICS . . . OH MY!

When sprinting into life, it is imperative to avoid oncoming traffic. The traffic can come in many forms: unhealthy relationships, financial crises, tornados, and pandemics, all of which are heading straight toward me. I collide with each one, somehow avoiding the total devastation each could bring. Determined, I pick myself up and continue toward the finish line of God's promises.

Thunder cracks as I walk into my apartment after a long shift at work. It's not raining, and I haven't heard of any bad weather predictions for the evening. I shrug it off as my imagination, put my phone on the dining table, and make my way into the kitchen. It's eleven o'clock, which means it's time for my favorite after-work snack: peanut butter. My phone blares an alert from the dining table, "Tornado warning in the area. Seek shelter immediately." *Tornado? But I'm alone.*

I fear dying alone. I've grown up with tornado watches and warnings, but usually when they happen, I am at work or in school. I've never been under a tornado warning and not had someone with me. I want to look out the window, but I am too afraid I will be sucked out of my apartment and land somewhere in my work uniform. I do not want to die in a tie and compression socks. I grab my love letter from Jesus I found at the Goodwill and jump into my bathtub. I pray, and I call my mother. "Mom, there's a tornado. Get the dog and Dad, and get in the shower." *There's a sentence I never thought I would say.*

The tornado touches ground 0.8 miles from my apartment. It decimates my town, destroying half of my high school. It annihilates the tiny church and school that was my childhood daycare. So much of my childhood is gone in seconds. Homes are destroyed, lives are lost. Some of us are without power, and some are left without hope. There is a heaviness and grief encompassing our city, but unfortunately, there is more pain to come.

My friends and I are without power. We get a room at the hotel I work at for several days until our power comes back on. In the meantime, I find a generator for my parents, who are also without electricity. I feel less like a daughter and more like a guardian, always ensuring their needs are met.

At work, my server assistant complains I am not tipping him enough. He disappears through most of our shifts to smoke and drink hot tea. He seems to have work confused for a hookah bar. I quit tipping him as much as I tip the other server assistants. You must work for money. It's a crazy concept. He yells at me in a language I can't understand.

"Look, you need to chill out or you're going to get yourself fired," I warn him.

About twenty minutes later, I am approached by security and my manager. "Ma'am, is everything okay? We heard something about a fire," the security guard asks me.

My server assistant has informed hotel security I am threatening to burn the place down. "No, I said he was going to get himself fired," I explain.

The security officer and my manager laugh. "Let me get a picture of your ID for the report, and don't worry about it," the security officer tells me.

A day or two later, I am told my server assistant is not happy with security's dismissiveness of his report and has gone to human resources. There is an investigation being made about my threat to burn down my place of employment. I am not an arsonist; I only date them. Luckily for me, the case is disrupted by a pandemic.

Before the country shuts down, there is a tension in the air at the hotel. People are wearing masks, and guests are canceling their stays. It has become solemn. "We're here on vacation because pretty soon this whole country is about to shut down, and then who knows what?" one of my tables tells me. I tell all my coworkers. Some of them believe me. Some tell me there is no way. People say they didn't see the pandemic coming. I did. I saw the panic. I felt the foreboding in the air.

The hotel furloughs all of us. Our manager hands us a piece of paper telling us to apply for unemployment. Some of my coworkers are in America on a visa internship. Their countries are closing their borders, and the hotel is kicking them out of their rooms. The rest of us stress over trying to pay our rents and mortgages. I watch as my place of employment casually throws us all away.

As the hotel tosses us aside, I throw myself into writing and creating online content. Fear consumes our country in different ways; some are afraid of the virus and their livelihoods, others fear each other, and some fear being ostracized for visiting their friends and family. I, on the other hand, fear becoming irrelevant. I see the pandemic and losing my job as an opportunity to become a better comedian. I've spent years on and off stage due to sickness or working the night shift. Now, there is no night shift and no leaving the house. I can write and create characters without any distraction, other than the plethora of strange men in my DMs.

I spend months creating content and writing new material, convinced that either my career will take off and I won't return to serving, or the hotel will bring me back by the end of the year. I collect unemployment until it runs out, and then I panic. The hotel is not calling me back to work, and America is afraid to return to live entertainment. Desperate, I reach out to my church for financial assistance. At first, it helps me with a light bill and some groceries, and then a woman from the church tells me, "Call the Baptist church. They are helping a lot of people."

I'm a Catholic. I am part of one of the world's wealthiest institutions. Why would I go to the Baptists? We're not even sure they're getting into heaven. This doesn't sit well with me. Eventually, I do something I thought I would never do, which is leave the Catholic Church. I leave it for many reasons: the greed, the theology, and the sexual abuse. I can no longer be a part of something I don't want to understand.

As the country opens back up, I find myself on every stage I can possibly get on. I take every gig, although most of the rooms are empty—well, emptier than before COVID. I am determined to not return to serving. I want to be a full-time comic.

One evening, I am at an open mic working on a bit I have written about my toxic relationship with my ex-psychic when I see a familiar face in front of me. It's Stephen, the magician who came to my high school chapel and shared his testimony with us. Because of him, I felt less alone in the world as a suicidal teenage girl. I introduce myself to him after the open mic.

"If you're serious, I'll help you. Here's my card," he tells me.

I call him the next day. He gives me notes for my set, and I go out that night and record myself and send him the video. I will take all the help I can get. I tell him I am not going back to being bullied by my server assistant.

"Well, alright, then. You are serious. I know some guys who can help you. They've got nothing going on. It's a pandemic," Stephen says. He introduces me to other magicians and comedy writers, and via Zoom, they help me build my set.

I perform in some clubs and show my father a video of me featuring in Arkansas. "Ashes, I'm real proud of you," he tells me.

I want to keep his pride coming. I email bookers, continuing to take every gig, but there's not enough. Comedy clubs are not opening, and now the hotel is bringing us back. I need to decide. Do I go back to working five nights a week in a cushy job with benefits and put comedy back on the shelf, or do I take a risk and work a part-time job with no benefits, no insurance, and chase the comedy dream? I'll take the risk. *No more hotel motel.*

CHAPTER 33

THE MEN OF
MY DREAMS

Determination is what separates the extraordinary from the ordinary. Some people are comfortable in their complacency, and others, like me, fear it. Determination accomplishes goals, but it also creates division between the driven artist and her former Driver's Ed teacher. The teacher doesn't feel it is safe for the artist to go out on her own. The teacher wants her to stay in "park," where it is safe. The teacher wants to be forever needed, and for me, my mother is that Driver's Ed teacher, afraid to give me the keys to my own life.

No matter how long I have been driving on my own, she will shout that I don't know what I am doing. She is not happy about my reluctance to return to full-time work and is not only vocal about it but is angry with me. "It's time to grow up. Go back to the hotel, or you'll be sorry," she warns me.

I refuse to accept my fate as a hotel waitress. *No, it's time I grow away from you.* Once again, I make the decision to live my life the way I want, like the healthy adult I am working hard to become. I try to establish boundaries with my mother, and this time, I quit calling her and I quit visiting her completely. There are mothers who protect their children from harm, and then there are mothers who harm their children. My mother is the latter. It does not matter my age; she will always hit me where it hurts the most.

My father sneaks phone calls to me behind my mother's back. He is not allowed to speak to me. He lies and tells her he is going to the store, and then he visits me at my apartment and we catch up. "I have something to tell you. It's getting serious with me and Myrtle. I want to leave your mother, and the three of us can be a family."

"Dad, would you really do that?"

"Well, I don't know. I would have to make sure I could take the dog, and I would miss my computer and my books." *What is wrong with him? This is an affair, not summer camp.* My father's problem-solving skills are incredibly disconcerting, but I empathize with him. *If Myrtle is still willing to see my father, she may have loved him all these years. Maybe she would have loved me more than my mother. Maybe she still could.*

I take another risk. I meet Myrtle in the parking lot of a coffee shop. She is happy to see me and tells me she is glad to have reconnected with my father. "How is your mother?" she asks me.

"Not good," I reply.

"She always was so controlling," she says, empathizing with me. It feels good to have another woman in my dad's life acknowledge my mother has failed us. "Your father said he has a heart condition. You know those are brought on by stress.

I think your mother is making him sick." I feel my eyes grow big. *Could she be making both of us sick?*

I feel guilty for going behind my mother's back and meeting the woman my father once loved. I know for her it could be the ultimate betrayal, but I don't care. Like a child, I want a new mom. Mine's broken.

I struggle with my family, and I struggle with my own relationships. I painfully learn men view celibate women as a challenge or a quest to be conquered rather than as a future wife. I had, of course, already suspected this, but I've always been a dreamer. I dream of many things. At night, I dream of the men who will come in and out of my life over the next several years. I dream of men from my past reappearing into my life to date me, and I am confused when they reappear into my waking life with false promises of love and a future. It's hard to determine which one is my husband when they're all the man of my dreams.

My dreams are also terrifying. One night, I dream of a dark figure with tentacles lying on top of me, choking me. I wake up scared and gasping for air. I wake up again from another dream of my father touching me in places I don't want to be touched. I keep this dream to myself because something must be very wrong with me to dream of such an awful thing. I dream of love and of horror, neither of which I understand. Confused as to why my love life and my dreams are in such disarray, I turn to a new type of therapy: podcasting.

There's a hunger for podcasting. Podcasts remind me of talk radio, which reminds me of the mornings my father would drive me to school and make me listen to Dr. David Jeremiah when I wanted to "Push It" with Salt-N-Pepa. Podcasting is where comedy is heading, and I have an idea. "I kinda want to do a podcast about breakups. I'd call it *I Got Dumped*," I tell my friend, Hannah, on our way to a show.

"Oh, I love it! Let's do it. We can start next week! We can use my studio," Hannah exclaims. Hannah witnessed the demise of my last relationship. She knows what kind of material I'm packing here.

CHAPTER 34

I GOT DUMPED

Hannah and I record from January to the end of November 2021. We take turns writing short essays on topics such as love, breakups, and relationships in general. We learn a lot about ourselves, and we share it into microphones for an invisible audience.

I often wonder how I come across to our listeners. It is clear I have problems, but at the same time, I am unapologetically aware of my own shortcomings. I share my heartache, and I share what I learn in therapy with the intention of healing others and sorting out my subconscious.

I reach out to another deliverance ministry. I am convinced something was missed with my former deliverance minister in that tiny church office. As my new minister prays with me, I have a strange thought. *I think my dad did something to me.* I am struck with terror . . . I do not have a memory of my father abusing me. *Could it be repressed? Or is this just fear?* Surely, this is an irrational fear; however, I tell Hannah and our invisible audience, "I have endured a lot of abuse in my life. It began in my childhood. I am beginning to believe that throughout my years of counseling, I have missed a memory somewhere or the Lord hasn't revealed it to me yet."

I know there is more to my story than what I have written in journals and scribbled into notebooks. Something happened to me when I was a little girl, and it has put a target on my back for abusive men. If I could remember and process it, I could heal, and "if I were completely free from abuse, I don't believe abusers would find me so appealing," I conclude. I don't know why, but I have a feeling my father may have done something to me.

I recognize I am a people pleaser. I bend boundaries in relationships with men because I don't want to hurt anyone, and I don't want anyone to hurt me. I don't leave toxic relationships quickly enough because I don't want to be a quitter. I share the story of the time one of the other bride scammers set me up with a guy from her gym. He took me to his high school reunion and duped me into smoking black tar heroin. Of course, I should have known when I saw the aluminum foil that this was not a good idea. I spent the night sick and miserable because I didn't want to tell a guy no and hurt his feelings, so I hurt myself instead.

The biggest self-realization I have is when I realize fear motivates my relationships. I tolerate abuse from men because those men tolerate my bladder condition. I don't see how anyone could love a woman who is hurt by sex. I put up with them because they put up with me. I settle in love because I have an unsettling condition. I am like my mother's castle, always settling.

I wonder if I have "daddy issues." I look at my relationships with men and look for the similarities between them and the relationship I have with my father. My father, like a lot of fathers, is emotionally unavailable. I visit him and my mother. He greets me, and then he leaves the room to play on his computer. He's always been this way. He was never a protector and never gave me any guidance in life. *Could I be attracting emotionally unavailable men because that is what I am accustomed to? Could I be searching for guidance and protection instead of love?*

I look at my life and my problems and decide all my antics were a desperate plea for my father's attention. I feel ashamed of myself. I blame myself more than my father. I learn to accept his unavailability and take the heavy stuff to God.

In between work and recording, I meet a man at my gym. His name is Lyon. He's tall, with big hazel eyes and bigger biceps. He's the king of Gold's Gym. He asks for my number, and I give it to him. I am not in a place for a relationship, and I know it. As attracted as I am to him, I regret giving it to him. I know the kind of men I attract, and he can't be good for me. If he was, he wouldn't be interested in this version of me.

He asks me to lunch, I tell him I need some time, and he says he understands. For the following nine months, he randomly texts me to check on me, and I consider his motives as genuine. But for now, I move on with my life as my parents' handler—that is, until I get a visit from death.

CHAPTER 35

COVID-TORIOUS

I am not feeling well. At first, I think it is stress. It feels like a cold, but it won't go away. I go to a walk-in clinic. The practicing nurse thinks it's a cold, too, and gives me a steroid. In a couple of days, I feel better.

I lie out at the pool and enjoy the summer sun, and then suddenly, it hits me. *I am not well. Something is wrong.* I take myself back to another walk-in clinic. "What are your symptoms?" the nurse asks me.

"Well, it started as a cold, then I got better, but now I feel worse."

"It sounds like COVID. I'm going to test you," she says, grabbing a swab. *I have been convinced I have had COVID every week since the pandemic started, and I haven't had it yet. Why would I now? I've dodged this bullet.*

I get into my car to drive back to my apartment and feel a dark presence with me. I pray, and I call Yay Jayme. "They tested me for COVID. I think I might really have it this time," I tell her.

I have an incoming call from the clinic. "You tested positive."

"Okay, what do I do?" I ask.

"Get some Robitussin." Within an hour my nose is burning. It feels like a UTI in my nostril. A friend tells me of a functional doctor who is helping COVID patients. I reach out and call him, and he orders me some supplements. Thankfully, Jayme drops them off at my doorstep. *I should be feeling better soon.*

The virus hits me hard. It starts with a sudden sharp pain in my right shoulder. I can feel it scorching its way through my body. I cry. I am scared and so thirsty. I chug water and Gatorade, but nothing quenches my thirst. I have had a fever for days, my bladder is on high alert, and I struggle to make it to the bathroom every twenty minutes. *This can't be normal.* I struggle to stand up. I feel so dizzy and lightheaded. This doesn't feel like the flu; this feels like poison.

I call Jayme again. "Go to your parents' house right now," she says. "You need someone to take care of you."

"I can't. They'll die," I explain. "I think I'm dying," I tell her in between tears. I feel a darkness around me, and I see a large-cloaked shadow standing in my bedroom doorway. I sense it is coming to steal me and take me somewhere, but for some reason it cannot get near me. It only stands tall in the doorway, menacingly, terrifying me nonetheless.

"Jayme, I am afraid. I don't understand. God gave me a promise. He said I would do so many things. This can't be the end."

"It's not. Keep your mind on what God told you. You gotta fight," she tells me.

It is getting harder for me to walk to the bathroom. I call an ambulance. The paramedics arrive and test my vitals, then tell me, "Your vitals are normal. This is part of the virus. We can take you to the hospital, but you're going to feel the same way and be in a waiting room. You are better here."

I stay home, and desperate for her love and care, I call my mother. I have always had my mother with me when I was sick, so I don't know how to cope with illness without her. She comes to my apartment and sits with me as I cry. She looks just as scared as I am, and I believe she's truly afraid of losing me. My mother loves me; she just doesn't know how.

She leaves, and the next morning, I wake up and I am coughing blood. I call the functional doctor, and he prescribes me ivermectin and some breathing treatments. It appears I have COVID and pneumonia. My mother picks up my medicine and a nebulizer for me. Unfortunately, the ivermectin does not help me. In fact, nothing helps me, but time. I struggle to recover as I take weeks off from work. My friends chip in and give me money and groceries to help me get through what I believe to be a brush with death. Lyon periodically texts me to check on me, and I promise him a lunch date as soon as I feel well.

It takes me eight weeks to recover, and once I do, I decide it is time I return to saving my family. My parents are falling apart, and they're also falling on the floor. When I was a kid, we were afraid of burglars. Now we are afraid of hardwood floors.

Early one morning, my father wakes up at around two-thirty. He has wet the bed. My mother wakes up to clean his mess and notices the fan on her back porch is on. She opens the door, misses her step, falls on the ground, and breaks her arm. I take her to the emergency room, where the doctors take turns asking her to describe *in her own words* what happened.

I am baffled. Who else's words would she use, my father's? I doubt that.

My father would tell them, "I don't know what happened. One minute she's standing there yelling at me. Next thing I know, she's on the floor yelling at me. Usually, I can walk out of the room, but this time I had to step over her."

My father is having multiple health problems. One night he gets a fever and tries to leave the house. "I'm going to the bar," he tells us. My father has never been a bar drinker. He is a stay-at-home-and-drink father. He also has memory problems and struggles to drive. I suspect Alzheimer's. I check his email and find more emails between him and Myrtle. I tell him to stop emailing her, and I reach out to Myrtle and tell her she must stop emailing my dad. He is not mentally capable of keeping secrets anymore. Something is wrong with his mind.

CHAPTER 36

JUST DON'T DO IT

Secrets and betrayal may hide in the dark, but eventually everything that hides in the dark comes to light. My father's affair in his late seventies is no different. I receive a phone call from my father, "Ashes, your mother left. She found the emails."

I feel a rush of panic hitting me in the chest. My heart races. I drive to my parents' house and park in their driveway. My father is on the back porch. "What happened, Dad?"

"I don't know. She wants a divorce," he answers me.

"Does she know I met her?"

"No, no."

My mother's car pulls up. I fear her and her wrath. She looks heartbroken. I pity her, and I feel guilty for having betrayed her. I must come clean. "Mom, I'm so sorry," I tell her.

"You knew?"

"Yes, I knew there were emails." I can't give her the whole truth. She terrifies me. She joins us on the back porch, and I explain my father's bad behavior. I tell her it was innocent. He wasn't going to act on it. It's not worth a divorce.

She watches me make excuses for my father, and then she looks at him. *"You,"* she says to him, then looks back at me as if there is something she wants to tell me. She turns her head and opens the door, disappearing into the darkness of her castle. *I know a secret when I see one. What did she want to tell me?*

Honoring my parents, much like changing boyfriends, is a part-time job. Sadly, their dog gets cancer and must be put down. She, like the rest of us, was always sick. When they return from the vet, my father opens an email from someone claiming to be an Amazon employee. Someone has hacked into their bank account and stolen $2,000.

When I call my mother, she is upset about her lost money. She calls it "this whole Amazon mess." I don't understand what she is talking about; I can't follow the story. This goes on for two days until she stops answering my calls. I am concerned, feeling something is not right. I drive to their house, and she is gone.

"Dad, where's Mom?"

"She went to the store to get some gift cards."

"That's weird," I say, speculating about what she had been doing.

My mother storms into the house while on her phone. She plops at the table and scratches codes off Nike gift cards. "Ashley, read this to me. I need to give this code to the man on the phone."

I start to read her the numbers on the card until I realize she is being scammed. "Mom, give me the phone." I take the phone and hang up on the scammer.

"Did you call your bank? Did you even check to see if money was gone?" I see fear flash behind her eyes.

"No, I didn't," she admits. My mother gave the scammer her driver's license number and the numbers to both her checking accounts. Unable to accept any fault of her own, she blames her problems on my father's emails with Myrtle. "Everything was fine until those *damned* emails."

I explain to her she needs to forgive Dad and Myrtle and move on. Fear, unforgiveness, and a bitter heart will steal more than any man or woman ever could. My rationale angers my mother, and often I find myself apologizing for reality.

While she stands outside the door of her physical therapy office, my mother falls and breaks her arm again. The following day, we take Dad to a neurologist for cognitive testing. The doctor asks my mother how things are at home, and she lies, "Everything is good. Real good."

I watch as the doctor hands my father various objects like a safety pin and a pencil, asking him to recall them. He struggles to remember. The doctor also has my father spell words backwards, and he struggles with that, too, but who wouldn't? I don't have dementia and even I would struggle spelling *world* backward.

The doctor orders an MRI, and two days later, my mother informs me he has been diagnosed with stage 1 dementia. "But, what kind of dementia, Mom?" I ask.

"He didn't say," she tells me.

"Well, you gotta ask him. We need to know what we are dealing with here." I need a distraction. It's time I take Lyon, the king of Gold's Gym, up on his lunch date offer.

CHAPTER 37

SANDWICHES AND
IFFY HEARTS

Love arrives in many ways. Sometimes it shows up on your doorstep in a brown box labeled "shoes," and sometimes it shows up as a man in a restaurant with a goofy smile and decent listening skills. Unfortunately, sometimes the shoes don't fit and sometimes the man doesn't either. It's not letting go of the shoes or the man that's hard. It's letting go of the idea that these things will work out and last forever—that is what's hard.

It has been nine months since the first time he asked me to lunch. He's never pushed me into meeting him. I hate when men push me into spending time with them; it's manipulative. Relationships should form naturally, but some people approach love with pressure, and I've learned those men can't be my boyfriends anymore. Lyon has a carefree approach with me. He texts me occasionally. He doesn't harass or bother me. There is no obsessiveness. He genuinely wants to get to know me over a sandwich.

For the first two dates, I am unsure of my feelings toward Lyon. I find him handsome and surprisingly entertaining. He's very dramatic when he speaks, raising his voice and gesturing. I giggle like a schoolgirl. I could listen to him talk all day and some nights, which I do.

I tell him I am waiting until marriage to have sex again, and he tells me, "I figured that because of your faith." He asks if we can do other stuff, and I can't tell him no. A part of me feels obligated to please a man despite my convictions. I bend my own rule and I become infatuated with him, but there is a problem. My bladder is not handling our long make-out sessions well. Something is wrong. This is new.

Usually, I can buy more time before this happens. I panic. *I am going to lose him. I need to go back into therapy. We missed something.* I tell Lyon about the rape trauma, I tell him about my bladder, and I ask him if we could pump the brakes. He encourages me to seek out counseling. He believes I have been running from something for a while, and this is a good time to work on things because, as he puts it, "You have someone with you who gets it."

I return to my therapist, Carrie, and I return to my psychologist, Lindsey. Lindsey teaches me that my body needs to feel safe and secure in a relationship. I don't understand. *Why don't I feel safe with Lyon? Why don't I feel safe with any man?* I am back to crying on the bathroom floor and asking God why this is happening to me. *I can't lose another relationship.*

I commit to therapy twice a week. Each day I journal and practice mindfulness. I am determined to heal. Lindsey tells me, "Healing is not linear. Be patient." It is hard for me to be patient. I feel pressure to get better quickly so I don't lose Lyon forever.

In therapy, I make an incredible discovery. I discover that I blame myself for being raped. I am angry with myself that I did not stay sober after sober school. I relapsed, and I got myself raped. They warned me it would get bad, and I didn't listen. I remember Alex the Terrible leaving me lying in the woods and thinking to myself, *Wait, come back. Tell me this didn't happen. Tell me I'm wrong.*

I shudder at the thought I would want him to return to me after violating me. I forgive myself. I let myself process the anger, grief, and regret. I recognize the rejection and abandonment I felt that night in the woods. *Is that what is tormenting my bladder—the fear of rejection and abandonment?* I discover a part of me has a victim mentality, and I work with that part and assure her she is strong. I am no longer a helpless princess stuck inside her mother's castle.

I reiterate to myself that I am safe and I am loved, but in the meantime, Lyon pulls away from me. "You need to focus on getting better. If you're worried about me and the relationship, we might not work out, and it could end in three months. Let's take some time off for now so this can become a long-term relationship." I want to believe him, but I don't. I know very well the sound of a man with an iffy heart.

I am exhausted. I feel rundown again. I reach out to my doctor and am diagnosed with long COVID. I am also in the bathroom every fifteen to twenty minutes with my bladder. I lose hope. I entertain the idea of suicide and make a to-do list. First, I need to decide how to divide my assets. *Should I leave my books to Hannah or Yay Jayme?* Next, I need to meet with a lawyer and draw up a will. *A lawyer would see the inch of gray roots in my hair and catch on to what I am doing. I would risk another hospitalization, and my insurance sucks.* Finally, I need to draft the *perfect* note. *It must be heartfelt and sincere. Something like, "I love all of you. I will see most of you later. I am still unsure about the Baptists. Love, Ashley."* Honestly, what keeps me from suicide is the to-do list. It's a lot of decisions, and I am just so darn tired. I'll get around to it another day when I am feeling better.

I am no stranger to dark places in my mind, but things are different for me than when I was younger. God gave me a word. *I will do so many things.* I can't stay in self-pity. I must keep moving toward the finish line.

I become aware of the unhealthy thoughts racing through my mind. I learn to stop them and label them. When I am worrying, I stop myself and say out loud, "Worry." When I catch myself fantasizing about a future that I don't know will happen, I stop myself and say out loud, "Fantasy." I am learning to take my thoughts captive so I am no longer a prisoner to them. I practice mindfulness and become aware of my breathing. Every morning, I practice focusing more on my breath and less on my thoughts. I read the word of God. I am rewiring my brain. My symptoms are lessening, and slowly, I am getting better.

I notice that once again I am always waiting by the phone listening for a ring or chime. Lyon is pulling away from me. It is hard to calm my mind when I am so afraid my bladder has destroyed my chance at love. We see each other for dinner, and I catch him staring at me from across the table. I can't tell what is going on behind those hazel eyes. I don't know if he loves me or if he's looking at me for the last time, or maybe both. At the end of the date, he hugs me and assures me, "Everything is going to be okay." Sadly, it is the last time I see him. He writes himself out of my story.

He may have given up on me, but I never give up on me. I wake up every morning and pray. I continue to practice mindfulness, journal, and take my thoughts captive. I tell myself over and over that I am being healed. I thank Jesus for healing me. I stop letting myself spiral into self-pity and despair. I tell myself my worth is not based on the opinion or the attraction of a man. I can let go and believe there is someone else out there for me who won't leave, and when I meet him, it will all make sense.

My symptoms decrease, and I start to have good mornings. Some days I have good mornings or evenings, and then some days are not good at all until eventually there are no more bad days. For the second time in my life, I am not chained to the toilet, but I have a new revelation: If my bladder condition is tied to sexual abuse and it originated in my childhood, what happened in my childhood?

I confront my mother. "Mom, my bladder is better after processing rape trauma. That leads me to believe my condition is related to sexual abuse. Did anyone ever touch me?" I ask.

"No, never. It was just me, you, your sister, and your father. No one ever touched you."

"What about a babysitter? You didn't mention a babysitter," I respond.

"You never had a babysitter." *But I did have babysitters.*

CHAPTER 38

PHONE CALLS
AND SHUDDERS

Healing comes to me gradually. It is not an overnight fix like some preachers in crowded churches claim. I fight for healing. I cry, I swear, I get angry at God, and I get angry at myself. I'm in a war only my health care team and my closest friends know about. It is ugly for months, and then it is beautiful. I can breathe again—for a little while, at least.

I am offered a new full-time job working the phones, except this time I'm not scamming brides and I'm not pushing cookware. I get paid to talk on the phone, and I have nights off for comedy again. I return to the comedy scene, booking gigs. Things are looking up. I write and rewrite my jokes. I practice onstage, and I practice in my living room. This time, I am determined to make it.

Everything is set up in my favor for me to succeed and to win. I also have the fuel of a woman who has just been dumped in my favor. As always, heartbreak catapults me into creativity.

I am sitting in my bedroom preparing for my workday when I receive my next heartbreak. My phone rings. It is my mother. "Hi, Mom," I answer.

"It's Alzheimer's."

My father struggles with finishing sentences, he is incontinent, and his motor skills decline. We need help, but my mother is the queen of denial. "Mom, we need a caretaking service. We need help."

She shouts at me, "No! I am not there yet!"

I don't understand. It's not about her. She leaves him home by himself while she runs her errands and goes to her doctor appointments until he calls me one day scared. "Ashes, where are you? I need help."

Afraid for my father's safety, I drive to their house. He explains he wants to take the lawnmower out for a joy ride. I am relieved but also angry at my mother's negligence. Another day he makes himself a grilled cheese sandwich, the first grilled cheese sandwich he's made for himself in forty years. It ends up being a burned piece of bread, but if it wasn't for the Alzheimer's, I am sure he could have figured it out.

"I'm going to change my hours at work, and you're going to start scheduling your appointments when I am off work. I will come sit with Dad," I say, taking the reins as my father's advocate.

I divide my time between work, helping my parents, and telling jokes. I also take a retreat with some other Christian comedians in Indiana. I listen as other comics share their testimonies. I want to share mine one day, but I know something is missing. I can't tell my story when I can't remember the story.

Another comedian asks to pray for me: "God wants you to know He is going to be very close to you this season. He is going to help you with your relationships," he tells me. I want God to tell me more about my career, but God is not a magic 8 ball. *Maybe He is going to bring Lyon back into my life.*

I come home and have three days left to myself: no work, no other comedians, and no parents. I can relax and just breathe, until my phone rings.

"Ashley, I need to have surgery. Will you take me?" my mother asks.

"What about Dad? Who is going to watch him? Mom, you can't keep leaving him alone."

"You are the daughter! I am the mother! You don't tell me what to do! You have been home for three days! Who doesn't call their mother in three days? Do you know how that makes me feel?" she screams.

"Mom, I am not responsible for your emotions," I explain.

"Drama, drama, drama! That's all you are. You act like you are so holier than thou and you don't even go to church," she shouts.

"I'm done," I hang up the phone.

I don't know what I mean by that, but something in me has clicked. I have sacrificed so much of my time to help her and my father, yet it's never enough. Nothing is ever enough. She takes and she takes from me. And she never gives me the only thing I want from her: her love. She'll have to figure her surgery out on her own. The next day, she texts me, apologizing and begging for my forgiveness. She agrees to get a caretaker. My mother is like a bad boyfriend. She uses me, hurts me, and then says she's sorry.

I take my mother to surgery, and her neighbor keeps an eye on Dad. There is a problem during her surgery, and she must stay in the hospital for a few days. The caretaker won't show up to work. This is very common in their industry. The caretakers don't care, so there is no one left to care for my father but me.

While my mother is gone, I become his nurse. I stay at their house, preparing three meals a day for my father, giving him medicine, changing his clothes, and changing his Depends. Some days he doesn't know who I am. His motor skills have declined so much, he is unable to button and unbutton his clothes. He forgets how to take his clothes and shoes off and on. I sit at his feet in tears in the bathroom, begging him to give me his foot so I can take his shoe off for him. *This is the saddest thing I've ever done.*

"Ashes, wow. I don't deserve this," my father tells me.

"Of course, you do, Dad." *Why would he say such a thing?*

My mother comes home from the hospital, and she is too weak to care for my father. I continue my role. "Ashley, Dad needs a shower. Would you?" she asks me. I shudder at the thought of bathing my father, but I can't tell her no. *Is it my fear of her, or is it my Christian faith telling me to "honor thy mother and father"? Where is the line? What are boundaries? Do I need those?* I put soap on my father's loofah and wash his back and feet. Yes, I need boundaries, and my father needs to be in a facility.

CHAPTER 39

DADDY'S GOT A GUN

My body is always getting my attention. I am still learning how to decipher what it is trying to tell me. Someone once told me, "When you can't say no, your body will do it for you." She's right. Maybe I wouldn't have so many health problems if I could learn to say no and create healthy boundaries. My body is healthy; it's my mind that's not.

My childhood friend, Kitty, invites me onto her friend's boat one Sunday. It's a beautiful day, and I could use the relaxation and a tan. We are on the lake when we pass a familiar-looking island. It's where I was raped. This is the first time I have seen it since I remembered the crimes committed against me on it.

"Last time we were out here, we saw a teenage girl sulking by herself. We almost pulled over to check on her. We thought someone hurt her, but then her parents joined her. She was probably just being a hormonal teenage girl," my friend tells me.

What if she was hurt? What if it was her parents that hurt her? I don't know why I would think such a thing, but I have convinced myself this poor teenage girl was being abused by her parents and probably needed my friend to check on her. I am the queen of worst-case scenarios. I would make a great soap opera writer. I'm looking at you, *The Young and the Restless.*

I leave the lake and return to work, but I am in so much pain. I can't stop going to the bathroom. A day or two later, I go to a walk-in clinic and explain my symptoms. I am given an antibiotic, but I feel worse. I reach out again to my urology team, Nurse Shelli and Lindsey. Shelli prescribes me another antibiotic, and Lindsey tells me this is common. I had a huge trigger seeing that island. "Will it happen if I go on the lake again?" I ask her.

"No, I don't think so," she assures me. I feel relieved. I don't want to live my life avoiding certain places or things because my body doesn't know how to act. Then again, I hope to never see that island again.

When it rains it pours, but for me it isn't raining—it's flooding. My life is becoming less of a life and more of a natural disaster. I am working when my phone rings. It's Kahn, my father's new caregiver.

"Hello?"

"Hi, Ashley. It's Kahn. Your father has a gun. Can you come to the house?"

"A gun," I repeat to her. Surely, she must be mistaken.

"Yes, your dad has a gun, and he won't give it to me. Your mother won't answer her phone."

Images flood my mind of my father shooting himself. I call the police and race to my parents' house, my fingers gripping the wheel. I begged her to get rid of the guns as soon as we got the dementia diagnosis, and she screamed at me, "No, no, no! I am not getting rid of the guns!" She has made this entire journey so much harder than it needs to be. Now, the man might kill himself. I almost don't blame him. She's been terrible to him.

"Ashes, I gotta get outta here. Your mother . . . she yells all the time. It's embarrassing," he would tell me.

"Dad, what if we could find you your own place, like an apartment? Would you like that?"

"Shit, yeah," he would respond.

I've witnessed her yelling and screaming at him. I've seen her lose her patience when he can't finish a sentence. "Well, get it out! Would ya?" she would yell. I would remind her he has Alzheimer's. Somehow, she is forgetful too . . . *Oh, the fentanyl prescription. That's why.*

I pull up to the house, and the police arrive within minutes. They tell me to wait outside. I wait in my car, and I feel my blood pressure rise. An officer comes outside and waves me into my mother's castle. My father sits on the couch, happy to see me. He is having a friendly conversation with the police who, according to him, "happened to be in the neighborhood."

I watch as Kahn hands my father a sandwich and takes out the trash. This is more work than she has done in the three weeks she's been caring for him. *What a show.*

"Ma'am, do you have any idea when your mother will be home?" an officer asks me.

"I don't," I coldly reply.

She's usually one of three places: Kohl's, the nail salon, or the pain clinic. Why she didn't answer the caregiver's calls is beyond me. She arrives and seems a little unsettled, not terrified like I was. Her lack of emotion baffles me. "I found my gun," my father informs my mother, like a child who found his favorite toy. The police inform her it is best to get the guns out of the house, and I take my father's gun collection to my apartment. Dad is safe, but he is afraid of her.

"You're in trouble," she says to him.

"Mom, it's time. We need to move Dad."

Somehow, she doesn't seem convinced. Two weeks later, she catches Kahn stealing her pain medication. Now, she admits to herself Alzheimer's is more than an inconvenience. It's a threat to life as she knows it. The two of us shop for memory care facilities together. This is by far not my favorite type of shopping with my mother, but I am ready to get my father safe.

In the car, my mother makes the strangest comment to me. "Your sister or her husband, I can't remember who, said your father molested your sister."

"Who said that?" I ask, demanding answers. *Oh God. Maybe he did do something to me.* I feel a lump form in my throat.

"I can't remember," she lies. Her head is full of tales, and her mouth is filled with lies.

"Mom, when was this?"

"I can't remember." *This is a huge accusation to not remember. What is happening? There is something going on here, and I don't think it's the fentanyl's fault.*

We continue our drive, deciding on a nearby facility, approved by my father. I pack up his books when I come across a journal. "What's that?" my mother asks me.

"Looks like a journal," I reply.

"Trash it. He's already written in it." I ignore her and pack it into the box. Meanwhile my father throws his toothbrush and a dirty sock into an old backpack. He's finally getting out of my mother's castle, and he's somewhat concerned with his dental hygiene. I'm somewhat concerned I have, in fact, missed a memory or, worse, a *secret*.

"Focus on the jokes," I remind myself. Everyone has something that distracts them in a crisis. For some people, it's another person, a relationship. For others, it's drugs or alcohol. For comics, it's the jokes . . . *and* drugs or alcohol. I am now getting feature work in some clubs—not many, but some. Throwing myself further into comedy is like taking medicine for me. I cry because watching my father's brain die hurts me, and I smile because making strangers laugh makes me feel "warm and fuzzy," as my fifth-grade science teacher would say. It's my heroin.

I am not feeling well. I think I am coming down with something, but I push through and continue to take shows. I feature, I emcee, and I do guest spots, taking every gig that comes my way because I need a distraction and something my mother can't take from me. I push out content on social media, and I keep writing. I take my father to the chapel on Sundays, and I cry at night from the heartache. I wish I had a husband to walk me through this, but at the same time I am grateful Lyon and I didn't last. I would not want him to see me like this. This is my train wreck and mine alone. I thank God for my broken heart.

I watch as other comedians continuously surpass me. My inconsistency throughout my career also breaks my heart, and I strive to prove to the world my worth. I am exhausted and fear I won't be able to stay onstage yet again. I am disappointed with my constant disappearance from the world due to my trauma and health issues. I reach out again to my therapist, Carrie, who explains to me God is always pulling for the underdog. That is what I feel like, the underdog. That is, until I make the list as one of the top comedians in my city.

PART 5

REMEMBERING

CHAPTER 40

I REMEMBER MONO

Denial. It's where I have always lived. Pam Tillis had a song in the nineties called "Cleopatra, Queen of Denial." I was young when it came out. I would hear it on the radio and sing along. Of course, I was a little girl. I didn't know what the song was about. I figured it was a silly song about a queen and her river.

My mother made fun of Pam, but I loved her. As I grew older, I became more drawn to songs sung by women who had their hearts broken by men. I wanted to be able to relate to the women and their songs. The sad truth is I related, except it wasn't husbands and boyfriends breaking my childhood heart; it was my father. I disassociated from and forgot what he did to me, but the signs have always been there. He was always sexually inappropriate and embarrassing, but I convinced myself he only had a perverted and weird sense of humor. He was harmless. I, like Pam, chose to float down a river of lies.

It is November 2022. It's getting cold outside, and the leaves on trees are falling, the grass is dying, and the air is thin and crisp. Many are decorating their homes in preparation for the holidays. I am usually one of those people, but not this year. This season is solemn. After all, this year has taken its toll on me. I've had many ups—the healing of my bladder, my new job, and even my name in a magazine—but I have had many downs as well. I have had downs that have brought me to my knees in sorrow and in prayer. I thank God for all of it. I thank Him for the wins, and I thank Him for the losses.

Sure, my father has Alzheimer's, but now he is safe in a home. His grilled cheese sandwiches are no longer a threat to my mother's kitchen. Yes, I had my heart broken by a guy, but I would rather him be gone than witness my coming undone. I prefer to handle my family's tragedy alone than to bring someone else into this made-for-TV drama. It isn't the breakup or the Alzheimer's that has me down this time. It's my health. What started as a mysterious bladder infection on the lake in the summer is now another bladder infection and a sinus infection. I've taken two rounds of antibiotics and am not getting better; in fact, I am getting worse. *What is happening to me?*

I've become aware of cycles and patterns throughout my life, and I choose to leave no stone unturned. I am aware I am stuck in a cycle of abuse with my mother, just like I was with Jack-the-Sorry Sack and Stan Duran Duran. I reason the abuse is making me sick. I reach out to Carrie once again, and we dig deeper into my relationship with Jack. I revisit the relationship, and in therapy, I forgive myself and I forgive Jack. I stop blaming myself for staying with him. It's not my fault. He was sick, I was sick, and I had been trained to be a prisoner of the unwell. It is over now. I have my own place, and I am safe. One day, I will meet someone else, and love will work out for me. Love is patient and kind, not suffocating or violent.

I forgive my mother for her emotional abuse and selfishness. I forgive my sister for not saving me from our mother and her castle. I forgive her for moving away and not being here to help me with our parents. I also forgive my father for not saving me from Jack and Stan and for not teaching me about love and respect. In the meantime, I visit my father, and I pray for him. I take his hands in mine and ask God to heal him, thanking Him that I have been able to honor my father in this season of his life.

"Ashes, wow. I am just so, so sorry," my father tells me.

"For what?" I ask.

"Well, you know . . ." his voice trails off, and he makes a strange gesture with his hands that looks sexual to me. *Surely not.* I laugh it off.

"No, I don't know. I don't understand what you are saying."

"Well, for when we would do what we would do," he explains. I feel seized by fear, and my body tenses. *Surely not.*

* * *

"We'll try another round of antibiotics, and I want to run a CAT scan of your sinuses," my new ENT informs me.

"And then what?" I ask her, knowing it isn't going to be an answer I want to hear.

"If you still have the infection by then, we might need to do surgery. In the meantime, I want you to see an immunologist. Something might be wrong with your immune system. There's got to be a reason you aren't responding to treatment."

I have the CAT scan, and it shows my sinus infection is gone, although I still do not feel well. "It feels like mono," I explain to the immunologist.

"Have you had mono before?" she asks me.

"Yes, twice," I reply.

"That's so rare it's almost impossible," she tells me. *That's what they all say.* It takes twenty minutes for the phlebotomist to draw all the blood she needs. My new doctor tests me for everything under the sun. In the meantime, I convince myself I have every autoimmune disease on the planet like the stable thirty-five*ish*-year old woman that I am. I anxiously wait for my results, and at night, I dream. I have a horrific dream of my father molesting me. *What is wrong with me?* I ignore it and continue worrying about my health.

Two weeks later, I return to the immunologist. "Well, you've tested positive for EBV." *Oh, God. Who is going to marry me now?*

"What's EBV?" I frightfully ask her.

"It's mono. And you are sure you had it twice? Those were confirmed with blood tests?"

"Yes, I am sure. Both were sent to the lab. Oh, I am so grateful to know what it is." *Praise God.* This doctor has never seen a happier thirtysomething mono-carrying patient in her life.

I call my mother. "Mom, it's mono," I exclaim. Well, it's mono and a bladder infection. I have a lot going on, but it's no longer cancer/AIDS/lupus/meningitis like I had suspected.

"Oh, no. Not again," she says. She doesn't see life like I do; there's no gratitude for her. Everything is doomsday. I am getting tired of my mother. I don't know why I call her to tell her every time I am sick. It seems ingrained in me.

Carrie believes at some point this served a purpose, but now I should be getting to a point where my mother doesn't need a constant report about my health. She is right, and she's worth every penny. I put up another boundary with my mother. In my father's absence, my mother now expects me to divide up my time between visiting my father, watching TV with her, and going out to eat with her. She does not see me as a daughter. She sees me as her assistant, her caretaker, and now her companion. I need to break up with her. *It's not working out.*

I visit my father. I feel guilty for not spending more time with him while I've been sleeping in and running back and forth to doctor appointments. My mother has given him a collection of greeting cards we gave him over the years. There are a few pictures of me as a little girl in that collection. He hands me the pictures and insists I take them home with me.

"No, Dad. You keep those," I tell him.

He grabs a greeting card and hands it to me. "Will you read this to me? I am having problems with my eyes." He's not having problems with his eyes; he's becoming illiterate. I grab the card from him. It is a card I sent him when I was trapped with Jack-the-Sorry Sack. I wished him a happy birthday and told him how grateful I was that he was my dad and was still alive, unlike Jack's dead dad. I tear up. I've been in therapy for weeks processing that relationship. *Something is happening.*

"Ashes, I am just so ashamed," my father says and hangs his head.

"For what, Dad? I don't understand."

"I only wanted to have fun," he explains. His response strikes fear into me again. I ignore the creepiness I feel and convince myself he is expressing guilt for not being a better father. Subconsciously he realizes had he been a better father, I would never have been in a violent relationship.

I have my bloodwork rechecked. The mono and infection are gone, but I still feel tired and rundown. I still have the bladder infection. I am on my fourth round of antibiotics. I am also in a lot of pain. I spend most of the day glued to a heating pad and pain medication. I fear hospitalization. I haven't had a bladder infection since I left Stan Duran Duran, and now I have had two in one year. *What is happening to me?* I blame my parents. As a child, they withdrew their love from me. They abandoned me, then trained me to associate sickness with love. *This is their fault.* I had no voice back then. Well, now I do. I call my mother.

"Look, Mom. We need to talk. I can't do this. I can't be your caretaker, your assistant, and your companion. I am your daughter. I have done so much for you and Dad. Most women my age cannot help their parents like I have you. It is time I live my life for me," I explain.

"Well, who is going to help me?" she asks in an angry tone.

"I don't know. Your church? A neighbor? But not me. I'm done," I tell her.

"Well, fine, then. I'll just kill myself," she threatens.

"It's not that serious, Mom."

"Well, where do we go from here? You just want to call me when you want to talk?"

"Yes, I want a healthy relationship."

Healthy relationships cannot exist with unhealthy people. It's not possible. I need to let go of my mother, but I can't. I try to reason with her and hope she can respect my boundaries.

The next morning, she calls asking me to help her take my father to his doctor's appointment. "No, Mom. I gotta work," I respond, maintaining my boundary.

Meanwhile, the pain from my bladder consumes me. I cry and pray God will show me what is wrong with me. I think of the card my father showed me and how coincidental the timing

175

was. I wonder if there is more. I feel a prompting from my spirit to search through my old notebooks and journals. I flip through the pages of each one, finding a journal entry of a dream I had when I first started comedy, of a man healing me from "the damage my dad had done from molesting me." I remember seeing a spirit in my bedroom at my parents' house and how at first glance, I thought it was my father coming into my room to rape me. I find another dream of my father molesting me after my breakup with Stan. *Are these dreams, or are these memories?*

CHAPTER 41

SORRY! NOT SORRY!

Betrayal. It looks different for everyone. Some feel betrayed when their partners cheat on them. Some feel betrayed when their jobs lay them off. Teachers feel betrayed when their students cheat on tests. And I feel betrayed by the two people who are never supposed to betray me: my parents, my own flesh and blood. I couldn't see it, but it was always there. It was always lurking within them and inside the walls of their house, waiting to devour and destroy me.

As I flip through old notebooks, I recall my father's recent apologies and expressed shame. I recall how much I hated him as a teenager and never wanted him to touch me. I would pull away, and everything he said annoyed me. As an adult, I have blown it off. I figure I was only a hormonal and angsty teenager.

My behavior wasn't anything out of the ordinary. It is common for pubescent girls to turn on their parents. I have felt guilty for my attitude toward my father. Now, as I read my journals, I remember the disdain I had for him. That part wasn't typical. I wasn't merely annoyed with my father; I *loathed* him.

As an adult, I feel uncomfortable hugging him or kissing him. I have a strange fear that he will get the wrong idea by my affection. I honestly believe every woman feels this way about her father. Now I question everything. Was he capable of committing the most heinous crime a father could commit? Could my father be a *monster*? As with all hard things, I turn to the Lord in prayer. I am convinced more than ever that a repressed memory, a trauma, a *secret* is making me ill. It's bringing me pain, delaying my destiny. I ask the Lord to reveal to me the truth. I am no longer afraid of the truth. I do not want revenge; I want healing.

I meet with Carrie the following afternoon. I am prepared to spend our hour processing some more trauma from my relationship with Jack-the-Sorry Sack, but I know I need to bring up my weekend. I tell her about the dreams and the vague apologies from my father. I expect her to blow it off and tell me dreams aren't something we can rely on, but she surprises me. "Let's process the dream."

We begin an EMDR session as I tell her about my dreams. EMDR is a type of therapy that uses eye movement and tapping on oneself to process emotions as a memory, or a trauma, is recalled. The idea is that sometimes our emotions surrounding an event can get lodged in one hemisphere of our brains, and by tapping or engaging in certain eye movements, the emotion is properly processed and healing can begin. We have used it for many sessions over the years, and it has successfully brought me healing each time. I talk about the dream, I tap my shoulders, and then . . . I remember.

It starts as an image of my bedroom doorknob. I feel the fear and dread I felt as a little girl watching it turn. I remember my obsession with locking doors in my parents' house, always afraid my father would walk in on me. I had to keep him out. I am flooded with despair. "AND SHE KNOWS," I sob uncontrollably. My mother, she knew, and she let him do it. I remember him stealing my innocence. I remember crying, "No, Daddy. No," and "I want my mommy." I remember him telling me we "had to do it" and for me to "be a good girl." I remember him walking away and me thinking to myself, *Wait, come back. Tell me this didn't happen. Tell me I'm wrong.*

I realize this is the same thought pattern that came up when we processed the rape trauma I experienced in the woods with Alex and the other boy. My therapist speculates if being sick kept me safe from my father's crimes. In unison, we both say, "Because he didn't want to get sick." It all makes sense. *This is real. This really happened to me.*

I call Yay Jayme and tell her everything. "Your mother," she says with a disdain in her voice. For years, I have told Jayme I thought he did something, but I had no recollection. I had no proof, but now I do: his journal. I want to read it. I drive to my father's memory care. I pray and ask the Lord to give me some confirmation. *Surely, I'm not making this up.* I dash my way through the hallway and find my father's apartment. My mother is sitting on the couch, and my father is in his recliner. I sit on the couch in between the two of them. *It's D-Day.*

"Dad, you keep telling me you are sorry. What are you sorry for? Did you hurt me?" I ask. My mother rubs my back. *Can she tell I know?*

"Gee, Ashes. No. I never hurt you." I look at the TV. They are watching a Spanish soap opera. My parents do not speak Spanish. My father spent decades taking Spanish classes on his computer but could barely order dinner at El OK Corral. I assume his Ecuadorian nurse picked the channel, and my parents are too lost in their own misery to notice.

The scene changes into a bedroom. A boy lies in bed as an older man walks into the room and oddly gets in bed with the boy. "Hey, he's got pants like I do," my father exclaims.

"Yes, he does. They're called pjs, Dad, and he's getting in the bed with a young boy. What do you think about that?" I ask.

"Well, you gotta get in there, do what you gotta do, and get out as fast as you can," he responds. *I think I am going to puke.* I get off the couch and make my way to my father's bookcase. I scour the shelves for that journal, and then I find it.

"What's that?" my mother asks.

"It's a Jesus book," I lie. Forgive me, Lord. "I gotta go," I announce as I head out the door and run back to my car.

In time, everything is revealed. We do not know when the truth comes out or how, but eventually it comes to surface. Like uncontrollable boiling water, overflowing and spilling out onto everything in its wake, my parents' secret destroys everything I thought I knew and loved. *The secret to their marriage is their secret.*

I am angry, heartbroken, disgusted, and in shock. I walk into my apartment, where the world around me feels distant and unreal. *This can't be happening.* I sit down on my couch, and I open that journal. I read the whole thing. I do not come up for air. It was a journal he kept from my childhood until my adulthood. He didn't write every day, which makes sense—he is terrible at keeping a commitment. He didn't need to write every day; he documented enough.

His journal entries were like mine, written as letters to Jesus. When I was seven years old, he wrote, "I have committed such a terrible sin. Please don't send me to the pit." On a day in 1998, he journaled it had been a "bad day" and said he was sorry for his "behavior." On the following page, he wrote that I was being admitted into drug rehab. There was a lot of attention toward me in that journal. There was more attention toward me than my sister and my mother. My birthdays were covered in stars and underlined with the words, "Ashley's Birthday." None of it made any sense coming from a father who was never there.

The fragments of my father's mind fall into the pieces and crevices of my own. Like a jigsaw puzzle, it all comes together. Those nightmares are not dreams at all. They are memories coming to surface. I call my sister.

"Laura, I've been having awful dreams of Dad doing things to me. He's been apologizing to me. I think he did something to me," I explain.

"Oh, I believe it. It was awful growing up around him."

"Mom says you said he molested you."

"I didn't say Dad molested me. I asked her if he was molesting you."

"Say, what?!"

"You were eleven. I came to visit, and you were different. You looked traumatized. You and Dad were having inappropriate conversations at the dinner table. He had you playing a computer game with him. I asked Mom if he was hurting you. I was behind her, and she was sitting at the kitchen table. She never turned to face me. She stared straight ahead and said, 'Your father is a good man. He prays and he goes to church.'"

She tells me more stories. She tells me of the time she was a teenager living in our mother's castle. She came home from school and smarted off to my father. He called her a name and started choking her until her face turned blue. Our mother screamed behind him, "Stop, you're going to kill her!" He let go of her neck, picked up the board game Sorry, and beat her with it head-to-toe until she broke free and ran out the door barefoot.

I remember that board game. It sat in my closet for years, held together by tape. I asked my mother one day what happened to it. "Oh, it's an old game, Ashley." It was an old game, an old game of revenge, and my mother held on to it like a souvenir.

I have all the proof I need. He was hurting me, and my mother protected him. Even animals protect their young. How could a mother ignore her child's cries? They should be in prison. My heart breaks. No one could help the little girl that I was. My emotions come in like waves, and sometimes I can't feel anything at all. I reach out to Nurse Shelli and Lindsey. I am still in pain from the bladder infection. I fear that it, combined with the emotional devastation, will kill me. Between the bladder infection, the mono, and the shock I can hardly move. It's the holiday season, and doctor's offices and therapists are about to close their doors for the year.

Lindsey encourages me to admit myself into a hospital if it gets too bleak. Shelli prescribes me another antibiotic and tells me, "It's not the answer we wanted, but it's an answer." She's right. I finally have the answer I've been searching for my whole life. I can get through this. I got through it before as a little girl, all alone. I can do it now as a grown woman, all alone. Each day I make myself clean one thing in my apartment. The tiny sense of accomplishment proves to me I can get through this, and I am getting better.

At times, I feel the dark realm of my childhood and my parents' house. It hits me like a breeze of wind. It is a type of memory I have never experienced. Other times, my mind races. I try to watch TV, but I can't hear an actor's lines. All I can hear is the sound of my own thoughts. *Did they know I repressed it? Did they think I just wasn't bringing it up? Even worse, did they think I was okay with it? Did my mother view me as a sister wife and not a daughter? How off the rails does this thing go?*

What torments me during the day does not stop at night. I wake up from the pain and anguish. In my sleep, I feel the sheer horror and betrayal of what he did. I only relive it for a fraction of a second before it wakes me. *My God. How did I live through this?* Another night, I wake up with my arms in the air as if pushing something or someone off me. Another night, I wake up frozen in terror. My memories visit me in my dreams. I reason my subconscious is finally releasing the trauma and pain it has safely stored for decades.

Like the journalism student I once was, I begin my own investigation. I call friends from my past and interview them. *What was I like as a little girl? Did I show the signs?* I call my childhood friend, Kitty, and tell her everything.

She responds, "You know what I always thought was weird? Your mother has this story about how the first time she saw me I was in Mass with my mother. My mother was bouncing me on her knee and your mother said, 'She looks like she's Ashley's age.' Well, where are you in that story? Where's Ashley?"

I know where I was. I was home with my father. My mother told me she couldn't take me to church on Sundays. She said I would scream and run around and tear the church books apart. Instead of putting me in a cry room, she left me home in the hands of my father.

She continues to tell me we spent most weekends at my house. We would stay upstairs, and I wouldn't let her go downstairs. If she needed anything from the kitchen, I brought it to her. I also made her sleep with me. I hid my friends in my room because if he touched them, too, I would lose them, and I made them sleep with me because I believed there was strength in numbers.

I ask Kitty to call her mother. I want to know what I was like to another mother. "Well, you were very sexual at a young age. It was in the way you walked and talked," she tells me. I am reminded of family week at rehab when I was seventeen years old. These were the things my father said he loved about me.

I reach out to my former fellow bride scammer, Lucy, and tell her. "It makes sense," she says. *That's what everyone says.* Lucy begins to have memories too. She remembers us talking on the phone and how I would make comments that my father was in my bathroom taking my trash out. My father was always wanting to be in my bathroom. He inconveniently needed to use my bathroom when I was in the shower. It's why I had to make sure to lock the door.

"Wait, I have another memory," Lucy says. "You called me once. You were whispering. You said you were in his computer room, and he did something, but you kept saying, 'I don't know what he did, but he did something.' I asked if he was drunk, and you said, 'Yeah, he must be drunk,' and that was the end of it. I think he may have touched you, but I am not sure." I had totally forgotten about this, but now I remember. I want my medical records.

I call my pediatrician's office and request my records. "I'll have them ready for you Monday," the receptionist tells me over the phone. On Monday, I drive to that office and grab my files. It's a folder filled with doctor notes and orders from my pediatrician and my childhood urologist. I read the notes from my first surgery, written by my urologist: "I think the child has a spastic uninhibited bladder, which we often see in these young girls. Fortunately, they usually outgrow this after several years." But I never did.

At three years old, I was suddenly wetting my pants and the bed after being potty-trained. At five years old, I was in the doctor's office nine times with various ailments and pains. Between 1989 and 1992, I had been to the doctor thirty-five times. I was always a very sick little girl. I stuffed heavy emotions inside myself, and my body did its best to purge them. He was always touching me, and she was always screaming at me. Where could a little girl go to hide but inside herself?

Six weeks go by, and the bladder infection is finally gone, but my symptoms have returned full force. My body remembers what my mind cannot. I haven't spoken to my parents since the day I grabbed my father's journal. I don't know what to do. I want to confront them, but also, I never want to see them again.

It's eight o'clock in the morning, and I get a text message from my mother: "Your father is crying for you. He wants to see you." Since we moved our father into memory care, the nurses have told us he walks up and down the halls crying for my mother and me. Before it was sad, and now it is sick. I decide I want to end this. I want to confront them both. I get into my car and drive to his memory care facility. My heart races inside my chest. I need to do this, not for him, but for me and the little girl inside me.

I get off the elevator, and he's sitting in front of it as if he was waiting for me. "Ashes, I'm so happy to see you."

"Come on, Dad. We need to talk." I gain momentum as I head toward his apartment.

"Slow down. There's strength in numbers," he says, laughing. He isn't making any sense, and it only causes my anger to rise.

His door is locked. I ask a nurse to unlock it and let us in. I sit down in a chair. "Your mother's got a boyfriend. I know it," he tells me.

"No, Dad. She doesn't have a boyfriend. We need to talk. Dad, the Lord has shown me you were coming into my room at night when I was little," I begin.

"I NEVER RAPED ANYONE . . . LEAST OF ALL, YOU," he shouts. *I didn't say anything about rape.*

"Dad, tell the truth," I say, pressing him.

"Ashes, no. I would never hurt you. How am I going to live the rest of my life knowing you think this of me?" *Have I made a mistake? No, I haven't.*

"Dad, tell the truth." I don't back down.

"Come on, now. Your mother says you can't get past this, and you gotta move on," he tells me anxiously.

"She said I gotta get past what?" I wonder if this is reality or the Alzheimer's.

"You know, *this.* Now come on; let's get out of here." I try my best to keep him on topic, but he keeps changing the subject.

I bring up his journal and the entry about his "terrible sin." He denies all of it. We walk around the memory care unit together, and he continues to fill my head with lies, just like so many other men in my life. I give up. He will never outright admit it. I should be grateful he apologized as much as he did. I head toward the elevator and look back at my father.

"You're coming back soon, Ashes?"

"I don't know, Dad." I doubt it. *I am Ashes no more.*

I leave the memory care facility and drive to my mother's castle. I pull up and park my car in the driveway. She is sitting in her dark den, as always.

"Mom, we need to talk. I know everything," I begin.

"Ashley, I don't know what you're talking about."

"Mom, Dad was molesting me, and I know. He's been apologizing to me, and I'm having memories."

"And you think I *knew*? That's why I haven't seen or heard from you? You thought I *knew*?"

"Yes."

"Ashley, I had *no* idea," she tells me as the house loudly settles, yet again.

I don't know what to say or think. She knew. *Did she disassociate from it like I did? Did it traumatize her?* She doesn't cry. She doesn't go into denial. She goes into self-preservation mode and continues to convince me she had no idea. And like the desperate daughter I am, I believe her. She takes me to lunch, and as usual, we go shopping, as if we are ordinary people living ordinary lives.

I am in shock, and I don't understand what is happening. *Did she really not know? How could she not know? Even if she didn't know, she's guilty of neglect.* My mother drops by my apartment twice the following week. We sit in silence. I tell her I am sad, and she replies, "OH MY GOD. I feel as though my whole world has turned upside down. I think I'm depressed. My blood pressure is through the roof!"

"Okay, Mom. I think we can both admit this is *way* harder on me."

"Right, of course."

On a Friday morning, she calls me and tells me she is having memories of what a pervert my father was. "He's more than a pervert. He's a child molester and a rapist," I explain.

"Ashley, I had no idea. I am so sorry. I feel like the biggest bag of shit," she replies.

I remember the wise words of my rehab counselor, *"Believe nothing that you hear and only half of what you see."* After several moments of silence, I inform her I need to start work. I do not hear from my mother over the weekend, nor do I contact her. I don't really want a relationship with her; I prefer grieving and moving on alone. I don't know if I can believe or trust her. I don't trust anyone, really. How can I?

The following Monday, she calls me at seven-thirty. "Listen. I don't believe you. I don't believe a word you've said about your father. I never want to see you or hear from you again. Don't come to my house. Don't text me. Don't call me."

"Okay," I respond. I am not angry or sad. I am grateful. She finally gives me the only thing I want from her anymore: *my freedom.*

She said her world has been turned upside down. That's not true. Her world goes on the same as it was before I confronted her. Nothing has changed for her. The only thing that has changed is that now I know and I will no longer work for her.

For years, I blamed myself for all the drugs, the psych wards, the sicknesses, and the bad boyfriends. I thought it was my fault. I thought I was forever indebted to them, but I was wrong. I had put my parents on a pedestal, a pedestal only God Himself could bring down. My parents were like a dead branch in my tree of life. Now, it's over for our family, but it's only getting started for me. I no longer need my training wheels.

CHAPTER 42

THE GOD WHO
SEES ME

I continue therapy until I have no more memories resurfacing. Unfortunately, I am still not feeling well, and I am still chained to the toilet. I reach out to my former deliverance ministers. They each pray for me. One of them suggests I reach out to an inner healing ministry, which helps survivors who have disassociated from childhood sexual abuse, like me, remember and heal from their trauma.

I contact the ministry and make my first appointment with Coach Esther Renee. In those sessions, memories come back to me. I remember my tiny fingers being slammed in doors, the screaming, and the crying. I remember when the only word I had for my father was *ouchie*. I remember him telling me to leave my door unlocked as a little girl, and I remember good things. I remember my pencil boxes and my New Kids on the Block poster, the skating rinks, and shopping at the mall. I remember the swings at the theme park, my tutu, and costumes for my recitals. I remember my dance bag and my dollies. I am proof that a little girl can be happy and hurting.

Eventually, I remember blaming myself for my father's "bad behavior," and I realize that is why I forgot—thinking of it only made me hate myself.

Grief leaves my heart, and I regain my energy. I don't feel stuck to my couch and my bed anymore. I can eat again. My father's sin is no longer the first thing I think of when I wake up. For a while, it's the second thing I think of until, eventually, it's hardly on my mind at all, other than when I write this book.

I dig through old journals for inspiration to write this book. I find an entry from 2018 when I documented a conversation between my sister and me about my birth. She informed me that before I was born, my family thought they were going to lose me three times. My mother bled throughout her pregnancy, I was almost born breached, and when I arrived the umbilical cord was wrapped around my head. I came into this world unable to breathe, and I spent my life fighting to stay alive. Death was always coming for me. It was there in the delivery room. It was there when another little girl choked me in preschool as I approached her for a well-meaning hug. It was there in my mother's castle when she sat on me and when my father defiled me. It was there when I was raped by people I trusted and when Jack was choking me. It was there in a factory and in a college classroom as I convulsed on the ground. It was there when I had COVID, and it came into my bedroom at night and tormented me in my dreams. It was always there waiting to take me out, but God was always there too. He was always near me, always watching me. He was always pulling for me and making a way for me out of the darkness. He never gave up on me even when I gave up on myself.

It is April 2023, and I write this story every day. I write it when I am sick, and I write it when I am tired. At times, it is written with a giggle, and at other times, it is written through tears. It does not matter what I feel; I still write. Nothing will stop the sheer determination of a woman who has been fighting her whole life to be alive. My bladder symptoms are subsiding, and once again, *I have good days and bad days until eventually there are no more bad days.* I am sleeping better. I am no longer anxiety ridden. I don't feel sick and rundown anymore. I feel lighter. My mind, body, soul, and spirit are healing.

The Lord continues to teach me a lot about myself. He teaches me I was once a little girl who didn't feel wanted, and as a result, I spent my entire life fighting to be seen, but God always saw me. My parent's abuse left me severely broken, but one by one, the Lord is putting all my parts back together as I continue my journey of forgiveness. For the first time, I am running toward life and not from it. I write this book because I want to share my story with you. I want you to know there's hope for me, and there's hope for you. *We can let the pain in our hearts break us, or we can break through.* I choose breakthrough. I hope you do too.

ACKNOWLEDGMENTS

Thank you, Jayme Zazworsky-Opincar, for being my best friend, my second sister, and at times, my unpaid counselor. If it weren't for you and our friendship, I wouldn't have had the courage to write this. You're the Ruby to my Sissy, the Romy to my Michelle, and the Mike Ross to my Harvey Specter.

Thank you, Lucy Cardwell, for walking me through this journey and consistently showing up for me. Our friendship is a treasure and has truly stood the test of time, much like our livers.

Thank you, Shelby McBay, for saving my butt so many times. I love you always, girl. We had some wild times. I wish I could remember them all.

Thank you, Peter Depp, for reading my story and being a (good) part of it, but most of all, thank you for dumping me.

Thank you, Hannah Slay and Dusty Slay, for supporting me, listening to my story, and letting me sleep on your air mattress. Thank you, Daisy, and Sam for being my playmates and reminding me what it is like to be young again.

Thank you, Kay Dodd, for being my mentor, my friend, and my comedy momma.

Thank you, Stephen Bargatze, for helping me become a better writer and comic, and for being this little girl's role model.

Thank you, Kelsey Mattos, for being the greatest boss ever throughout all of this. Our coffee chats sure took a turn, didn't they?

Thank you, Samantha Martin-Davis, for being my first editor. I appreciate your honesty, your candidness, and your willingness to read this coworker's lengthy cookbook.

Thank you, Coach Esther Renee and R.E.A.C.H. Freedom International, for your ministry and all the work you have done for me and other overcomers. Now, put me in that book club, girl.

Thank you, Above & Beyond Christian Counseling and Evelyn Benjamin, for ministering to me and praying for me. We knew there was something missing, girl and man, did we find it!

Thank you, Jansen Bagwell, Father Dan Reehil, Susan Skinner, Shawn Sulak, and Whole Catholic Coaching. This journey really began with all of you.

Thank you, Carrie Bock and By the Well Counseling, for pressing in, never judging me, and allowing me to make my own (few) mistakes.

Thank you, Rochell Burton, Lindsey Colman McKernan, and my team at Vanderbilt for never giving up on my care and sticking by my side all these years. It's not the answer we wanted, but it's an answer, finally.

Thank you, Elizabeth Maynard-Charlé, Matt West, Emma Sherk, and the team at Dexterity, for taking a chance on this first-time author and making one of my many dreams come true.

And finally, thank you to all my exes. You helped me write an incredible story. I'm so glad we never worked out.

ACKNOWLEDGMENTS

I would like to acknowledge the book *Cleaning Up Your Mental Mess* and its author, Dr. Caroline Leaf, whose teachings on neuroscience helped me rewire my thoughts and renew my mind.

I would like to acknowledge the book *You Are Not Your Pain* by Vidyamala Burch and Danny Penman, which provided me with additional mindfulness skills and practices that helped regulate my nervous system.

I would like to acknowledge the book *The Body Keeps the Score* by Bessel van der Kolk, which brought me to a deeper level of understanding regarding trauma and the mind-body connection.

I would like to acknowledge the book *Boundaries* by Dr. Henry Cloud & Dr. John Townsend, which helped me understand the fundamentals of boundaries and how they can heal and prosper our lives.

NOTES

1. Ashley Brooke (Corby), *I Got Dumped* Podcast, July 19, 2021.
2. *The Golden Girls,* season 4, episode 16, "Two Rode Together," directed by Terry Hughes, aired February 18, 1989, on NBC.
3. *Turning Point with Dr. David Jeremiah*, DavidJeremiah.org, 1982.
4. *Saturday Night Live*, season 21, episode 11, "Spartan Cheerleaders," directed by Don Roy King, aired January 20, 1996, on NBC.
5. Matthew 18 (New American Standard Bible).

ABOUT THE AUTHOR

Ashley Brooke is a comedian, writer, research manager, and an avid shoe collector. She has also been a waitress and an administrative assistant, and for one day, she was a door-to-door salesperson. She was awarded as one of the best comedians in Nashville, Tennessee, by *Nashville Scene* in 2022. She is the first female in Nashville to make the list. Ashley has been interviewed by *VUMC Reporter, Interstitial Cystitis Network,* and *NashvilleVoyager* regarding chronic illness, trauma, and her journey into comedy. Ashley holds a B.A. from Western Kentucky University in broadcasting. She is single and lives in Nashville with zero cats, despite the urging of some of her friends. You can visit her website at www.missashleybrooke.com.

Made in the USA
Columbia, SC
10 June 2024

36429486R00129